Creative Quilting

with

Kids

Maggie Ball

Published by

krause publications

The World's Largest Hobby & Collectibles Publisher

700 E. State St.
Iola, WI 54990-0001
Telephone 715-445-2214
www.krause.com

Please call or write for our free catalog. Our toll-free number to place an order or obtain a free catalog is 800-258-0929 or please use our regular business telephone 715-445-2214 for editorial comment and further information.

Library of Congress Catalog Number: 00-110083

ISBN: 0-87349-231-5

Printed in the United States of America

Quilt Photographer - Mark Frey, Yelm, Washington

The following trademarked or registered companies or product names appear in this book:
Berol®, Coats and Clark®, Crayola®, Createx™, Deka®, Delta Fabric Dyes®, DMC®, Marvy™, Nasco Life/Form®, Olfa®, Omnigrid®, Pellon®, Pentel Fabricfun™, Safety-Kut™, Scribbles®, Speedball®, Steam-a-Seam 2®, Styrofoam®, Ultimate Marking Pencil for Quilters™, Versatex®, Warm and Natural®, Wonder-Under™.

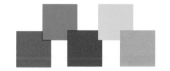

Dedication

I would like to dedicate this book to all young quilters and the teachers who patiently nurture them in the creative art of quilting.

Acknowledgments

Where do I begin? There are so many people to thank for all the support and encouragement I have received during the long process of writing this book. Many contributions have been gratefully received:

* Wendy Simon initiated me into the joys of quilting with children by involving me in the Wilkes Elementary School quilt project. Her enthusiasm and experience were an inspiration to me, and we worked well together. As a result of our success, I started writing this book.

* Diane Ross took an interest in my work, encouraged me to write the book, and told me to persevere in my search for a publisher.

* The staff at Doheny Publications Inc. especially Marilyn Doheny whose energy and positive attitude kept me on track. It was a pleasure to work with Mark Frey, who successfully captured the delight of the children on film, as well as all the small details, in a relaxed and seemingly easy way.

* Paul Kennedy, acquisition editor at Krause Publications, and Barbara Case, my project editor, were particularly helpful and patient.

* Support and words of wisdom from Margaret Miller and Cindy Walter were much appreciated.

* Many Bainbridge Island teachers, staff, and parents at Wilkes Elementary School, Blakely Elementary School, and The Family Classroom gave me a warm welcome, volunteered their time, and made appreciative noises as the projects were completed. Those making outstanding contributions are named as project participants at the end of the book. Special thanks go to M.J. Linford, whose artistic talents, rapport with the children, and sense of humor enabled us to tackle challenging projects and taught me much. In the face of difficulties she maintained her faith in the children and me, and we all came through with flying colors.

* My family and friends kept me going through hectic times and their support was vital to the completion of the quilts and the book. Many quilting friends, some who were barely acquaintances, jumped in to help baste and quilt the quilts. Joanne Bennett receives the grand prize for the many cheerful hours she willingly did whatever I asked. Nonquilting friends who provided much needed spiritual backup were my church and choir friends, book club (Wine, Women, and Books), and my gardening group (Whacky Weeders). My husband Nigel and my children Hazel and Thomas patiently tolerated my one-track quilting mind, taught me basic word-processing skills, sorted out my computing problems, and offered their critical opinions freely!

* Last, but not least by a long way, all the children who participated in the quilt projects. My desire to share their smiles, excited eyes, appreciative responses, and hard work has resulted in this book.

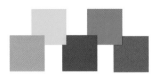

Table of Contents

Chapter Four - Projects 36

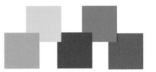

This book aims to inspire and encourage the sharing of the quilting tradition with children. I hope the projects described will serve as a springboard from which you will develop your own ideas and enjoy the immense rewards of working with children.

I decided to write this book in 1994, after the over-whelming response to a quilt auction fundraising event at my son's school. My quilting friend Wendy Simon and I spent five months working with every class at Wilkes Elementary School, Bainbridge Island, Washington. Under our guidance, all the children and teachers made 21 quilts, eight of which appear in this book, for the auction that raised over $14,000. The enthusiasm and energy of the children throughout was amazing. The project fostered teamwork and gave each class a great sense of achieve-ment. All of the 503 children and the 20 teachers partici-pated, as well as over 50 parent volunteers and many of our quilting friends. About a dozen local businesses pro-vided financial or material support.

The original goal of the Wilkes School quilt project was for each class to create a quilt to be auctioned at the fundraiser. I rapidly realized that the educational value of what we were doing was much more important than the auction. The children were extremely proud of their work

and the positive effect of their sense of achievement was noticeable throughout the school. This was an unexpected spin-off that delighted the principal and teachers. The auc-tion was the incentive that started the whole thing and gave us a deadline. As far as I was concerned, as long as we broke even I didn't mind how much money we made because the children had already benefited enormously from the experience. The money raised was used to fur-ther benefit the children and expand their educational hori-zons.

My experiences at Wilkes proved invaluable when I began more school quilt projects in 1997 at Blakely Elementary School and the Family Classroom, both on Bainbridge Island. These projects were thoroughly docu-mented photographically and are featured in this book.

At Blakely Elementary I collaborated with the art teacher, M.J. Linford, and we worked with 14 classes, making a total of 16 quilts. M.J.'s artistic talents and teaching skills enabled us to try new techniques not used in the Wilkes project which I would not have dared to attempt on my own! The projects were tailored to include skills taught in the art curriculum and were appropriate for each grade level. For example, the paper cutting unit in the second grade (eight and nine year olds) art program was

extended to include cutting paper snowflakes to make snowflake prints on fabric. Fifth graders (ten and 11 year olds) always study printmaking, so they cut their printing blocks and printed on fabric for their quilts. At Wilkes, Wendy and I collaborated with 20 teachers and scheduling was difficult. This was not a problem at Blakely, where I was working with one teacher using art class time already planned.

In the Family Classroom, there were 50 children between the ages of six and ten with two teachers in an open plan setup. It was a challenge to design projects suitable for the mixed age range and ability. I visited the classroom twice a week for three months and we made five quilts. The teachers approved the projects and had some input choosing a theme that integrated with the curriculum, but for the most part, I worked independently with the children. Like the Wilkes project, all these quilts could not have been completed without the parent volunteers assisting in the classroom and the quilting friends who helped to piece, baste, quilt, and bind.

For all the schools, the projects began by presenting a small quilt show to each class. The show was adapted for each grade level and included some historical background. The children responded enthusiastically, eager to ask questions and tell me about quilts they have at home or relatives who quilt. When an 11-year-old boy tells you, "That was a really cool presentation. Your quilts are great," you feel enormously satisfied!

Next the quilts were planned and the materials were selected and prepared. The range of capabilities of the classes meant that a variety of techniques were adopted. Many children drew or printed on fabric blocks with fabric crayons, markers, and paints; several classes used iron-on Steam-a-Seam 2 or Wonder-Under for fusible appliqué, and other children were taught how to hand stitch patchwork pieces and do simple embroidery embellishment. Three classes also hand quilted their quilts. The time we spent with each class varied according to the techniques we used. In some cases, for example, when the children drew on the blocks, just one or two class sessions were necessary. The most time-consuming was teaching children how to hand stitch.

When the children's work was completed, we assembled the quilts. We always included every child's work. Seeing their faces and listening to their responses was one of the most wonderful rewards for all our efforts. They loved to pick out their blocks on the quilt and admire their work. The enthusiasm was ever present at all grade levels from kindergarten to fifth grade. As the quilts progressed, the children greeted us in the school hallways and around town, eager to know how their quilt was coming along. "Is it finished yet?" "When can we see it?" "When are you coming to our classroom again?"

The completed quilts were displayed to be shared and enjoyed by all. At Wilkes the quilts were exhibited in the school gymnasium for the auction and in local shop windows during the week preceding the auction. At Blakely the hallways were decorated with quilts during the school

barbecue and proud children brought their parents along to see their work.

Children's quilts bring smiles to those who see them. I wish young people's quilts would be displayed at every quilt show and that the children would be rewarded by adult recognition of their work. The United Kingdom is leading the way with a national group of Young Quilters, organized by The Quilters' Guild. The members receive a quarterly newsletter and can attend workshops and activities organized at a regional level. Other European countries are following suit. I would love to see more countries copy the example set by the United Kingdom, where there is always a children's quilt category at the big national quilt shows.

There are all sorts of excuses to make quilts with children! You may like to celebrate some local or historical event, a special wedding anniversary, or birthday. Maybe a teacher or principal is leaving. A quilt, made by all the children would be a wonderful gift. Perhaps you would like to make the quilt as a fundraiser, to be raffled or auctioned. There are always needy people in the community for whom the gift of a quilt would be wonderful. Most hospitals have programs to help needy mothers, and small quilts for underprivileged or premature babies are greatly appreciated. Such a project would also teach the children about reaching out to those less fortunate. Perhaps your church needs quilts for the nursery, a banner, or an altar covering. Of course, stuffed animals and dolls love little quilts!

Most local quilt groups are involved in community projects and quilters love to share their work. They may also provide financial sponsorship. Both my local groups, Bainbridge Quilters and the Kitsap Quilters' Guild, donated money for supplies for the Wilkes project, and some quilters gave us fabric as well as much moral support and their time helping to make the quilts. At Quilters Anonymous, the large quilting group in Western Washington, I asked for help to quilt ten of the Blakely and Family Classroom quilts. Enthusiastic volunteers, some barely acquaintances, took all the quilts.

Quilting is not a subject normally incorporated into the school curriculum but there is much that children can learn from the history of quilts and the creative process. All sorts of disciplines may be integrated. Math, library research, writing, and the social skills required to work as a team are utilized, in addition to providing the opportunity for original art and the development of fine motor skills. I can guarantee that you will be richly rewarded for your efforts and that you and the children will have an exciting and enriching time.

I hope this book will inspire you - as a quilter, teacher, or nonquilter with little experience - to participate in passing on the heritage of quilting to the next generation.

Chapter One
Starting

PLANNING AND SETTING GOALS

Quilting with kids is fun and rewarding, but for the best results, your project needs careful planning. Don't be put off by all the "stuff" you might think you need. You may start children hand piecing blocks or drawing on fabric without a lot of special tools. Rotary cutters and boards are recommended and save time when cutting fabric, but are not essential for beginners working on small projects. Go to a quilt shop and enjoy the fabrics, and purchase just a few quarter or half-yard pieces of darks, mediums, and lights to get started. You may use any 100% cotton scraps you have at home too. Don't be afraid to let the children play around with the pieces and make their own designs. There is no right way, just plenty of techniques to make the job easier and more economical with fabric. Lack of technical knowledge shouldn't prevent you from the fun of making quilts. If you've never quilted before and you want to make a group quilt - at school, church, scouts/guides, camp, or with friends - you may choose to enlist some help from a quilter. If you are a quilter, you should already have most of the general supplies.

You will discover that you are not just teaching children about quilting, you are providing them with the opportunity to express themselves artistically. We included every child's work and it was not possible for a child to "fail." Just as children can write wonderful stories without being able to spell accurately or construct grammatically correct sentences, they can make wonderful quilts too - so give them a chance!

Think carefully about what you would like to achieve and ask the following questions to help you work out your project goals.

- Do you want to work with individual children, small groups, or large groups?
- Do you want to educate children about the history and different types of quilts?
- Do you want to make a bed quilt or a wall hanging?

- Do you have time constraints, or is the project open-ended?
- How much time per session do you have to work on the project?
- With what age group will you be working?
- What will be the theme or topic for your quilt?
- For a school quilt, does the theme complement the curriculum?
- What techniques will you use in the project?
- Are these techniques appropriate for the skill levels of the children?
- What is your skill level?
- If you plan to work with more than six children, do you have a helper?
- Do you need additional volunteer assistance?
- Do you have the support of the teacher or group leader?
- Do you need financial sponsorship to obtain materials for the project?
- Will the finished product be exhibited?
- Is the quilt being made for a special occasion?
- Will the quilt be a gift or a fundraiser?
- Are your goals realistic?

Make notes to record your ideas. *Thorough preparation is the key to the success of your project.* Time spent ensuring that your plans are complete is worthwhile. Shortage of materials and lack of organization will cause frustration for you and the children. Draw up a timetable, planning each session in detail. Make sure you allow enough time to prepare all the materials and that your volunteers are trained and reliable.

Each project in Chapter Four lists the number of sessions required, assuming 40-minute sessions unless otherwise indicated. Sometimes projects and preparation take longer than anticipated, or unexpected problems arise. Children work at different rates, so be prepared and ask those who work efficiently to help those who are slower. Be flexible, be realistic with your deadlines, and try not to hurry. Then you will be able to enjoy the entire project without putting undue pressure on the children or yourself.

Maggie and M.J. schedule and plan classes.

Group Quilts

If you will be working with a group, you'll need to know:

- The number of children in the group.
- The age and skill level of the children.
- The person responsible for the project and the availability of volunteers to help.
- How much time you will be able to spend with the children.
- The source for the materials for the project.
- The theme of the project.
- The techniques you plan to use.
- What materials you need.

Time may be a major constraint for a school project. Older children tend to have a more rigid curriculum with less time for special projects. However, your project will be rewarding, promote teamwork, interdisciplinary study, and a positive sense of achievement. At Wilkes School, Wendy and I had a warm reception from the teachers. Some, who were skeptical at first, soon became excited when they saw the results in other classes and the way the children responded.

Individual Projects

If you are working one-on-one with a child, scheduling should be straightforward and you will probably be fairly flexible. The chances are that you are a quilter with experience, a fabric stash, and ideas. For groups of children each working on their own projects you need to ensure:

- At least one adult helper for every six children.
- All the children have the means to obtain the necessary supplies.
- The techniques used are appropriate to the skill level of the children.
- Adequate time is allowed.

For individual and small group projects, it is easier to involve the children in every stage, including the preparations, and to have longer, more flexible sessions. A field trip to buy fabric is a good way to start, and you will enjoy the children's enthusiasm and excitement.

Choosing a Theme

For classroom quilts, try to select a topic that can be integrated into the curriculum, and involve the children as much as possible at all the stages. The children might research the topic, use their artistic and fine motor skills, and help with the mathematical calculations in the arrangement of the blocks, the size of borders, and the size and number of sashing strips.

If you are not working in a school, choose a subject appropriate for the particular group and the interests of the children.

If you are still short of inspiration, a trip to a fabric store may help. There are many theme cotton fabrics that can be used for borders and quilt backs.

Popular topics include:

Antarctica	Our Community
Marine Life	Our State
The Coral Reef	Our City
Endangered Species	Our Country
The Rain Forest	Our Solar System
Hands	Around the World
Hearts	Costumes Through
Teddy Bears	the Ages
My Friends	Ancient History
All About Me	Mythology
My Family	Natural History
Poems	Geometric Patterns
Family Tree	Farm Animals
Our School	Zoo Animals
Holidays	My Favorite
The Seasons	Storybook
Local History	Traditional Quilt
Special Events	Blocks
The Garden	Design Your Own
My House	Quilt Blocks
My Pet	National History
Modes of Transport	(e.g., to commem-
Architecture	orate an event)

Choosing a Technique

The creative possibilities are endless, and you can be successful using a variety of techniques. Do you want to teach children to sew, or use children's artwork to make a quilt? The techniques used in the projects in this book are listed below with brief notes to help you decide which are the most appropriate for the skill levels of your children and the time available.

Illustrations and writing on fabric. The projects are clean and easy and the children can usually complete their work in as little as one or two sessions. Suitable for all ages.
Printing and painting on fabric. These projects require the use of paint or ink, so they may be messy! For the fish prints and reverse stencils printing projects, the children can usually complete their work in one or two sessions. Block printing is a longer project, requiring the use of sharp cutting tools, so it is not recommended for children younger than ten years.
Fusible appliqué. Projects range from simple, where young children may cut out a single shape (e.g., hand or heart), to complex, for older children, where multiple pieces are fused to create a picture.
Hand sewing patchwork, appliqué, and embroidery. Challenging, but don't be put off - it's fun! I recommend at least one adult per six children, eight years or older. Six to eight year olds can sew, but require a lot of individual attention. Preparation and project times are often lengthy. It is a myth that girls are better at sewing than boys!
Hand quilting. Challenging and time-consuming but the kids love it! I recommend at least one adult per six children, eight years or older.

Machine sewing. Suitable for individual and small group projects. Not recommended for children under ten years.
Designing quilt blocks. Easy paper project involving simple geometry. Quilt project in which the children arrange fabric shapes to create their own blocks.

Some techniques require special supplies and these are itemized for each project - see Chapter Four. Read and follow the manufacturer's directions and try to use non-toxic products. More than one technique may be used, and embellishments with embroidery, beading, buttons, sequins, etc. will add extra pizzazz to your quilt.

GENERAL SUPPLIES

This is a list of useful supplies but they are not all required, so if you are new to quilting, don't feel overwhelmed. Each project has a supplies list but some of these general supplies are assumed and are not listed every time. The most timesaving tool is the rotary cutter used with a cutting mat and a 6" x 24" (15 x 60 cm) quilters' ruler. Make sure the blade is closed when the cutter is not in your hand. *Rotary cutters are very sharp and are off limits for children without strict supervision.*

- Sewing machine
- Iron and ironing board
- Rotary cutter, 45 mm
- Cutting mat, 17" x 23" (43 x 60 cm)
- Quilters' ruler, 6" x 24" (15 x 60 cm)
- 15" x 15" square (nearest metric size 31.5 x 31.5 cm)
- Ruler, 12" (30 cm)
- Sewing scissors
- Paper cutting scissors
- Graph paper
- Gridded template plastic
- Cardboard
- Measuring tape
- Sticky labels
- Plastic bags for storage
- Pencils
- Variety of fabrics
- Freezer paper
- Fusible webbing
- Batting
- Quilting needles, size 7 or 9
- Embroidery needles, sizes 3 to 9
- Regular needles and pins
- Embroidery hoops, 14" for individuals
- Quilting frame for group quilts
- Thread
- Beeswax
- Old dessert spoon
- Thimbles (children have small fingers)
- Marking pencils or chalk pencils
- T-pins for basting
- Safety pins
- Seam unripper
- Masking tape

TIPS FOR SUCCESS

- Adapt the projects and ideas in this book to your own needs and the interests of the children.
- Include every child's work. If children are absent, go back another day and work with them individually so that they can contribute to the project. Everyone wants to participate.

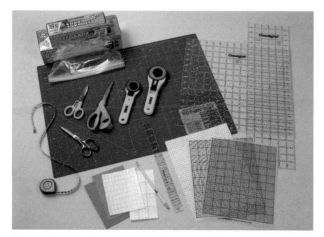

Measuring, cutting, and template supplies and tools.

Quilting supplies and notions.

⚜ Prepare extra supplies in case of disasters. For example, for a class of 30 children illustrating quilt blocks, cut four extra blocks.

⚜ Carefully plan the total number of blocks for the quilt. Additional title or name blocks may be added to make assembling the quilt easier. See page 30 for help with this.

⚜ For some projects, the children will be able to work independently after the initial session. Offer this as a reward when other assignments are complete. Children may hand stitch while listening to stories read aloud.

⚜ Do not allow the children to take incomplete work home - it will disappear!

⚜ The children will be eager to know how their quilt is progressing. Show them the quilt top before it is quilted and share as many of the stages as possible.

⚜ Set a project deadline. If possible, use an incentive such as an exhibition date.

⚜ Celebrate the completion of the quilt and give the children the opportunity to proudly share their creation with family and friends.

⚜ Arrange a follow-up project so the children have something to take home to remind them of the project. You'll find suggestions in Chapter Four. Instead of making one large quilt, individual blocks sashed and bound in the same fabric may be made into small quilts. Hang them together to appear as one big quilt, but after the exhibit, allow the children to keep their own blocks.

⚜ Photograph the children with the quilt so they can each have a picture.

⚜ Be flexible, relax, and have fun!

Introducing Children to the Joy of Quilts

The First Meeting
Children love special presentations and will respond with warmth and enthusiasm. Their observations and compliments are wonderful. You will be well rewarded for your efforts. If you are a guest artist, introduce yourself, briefly telling the children how long you have been quilting and why it gives you so much enjoyment. By the end of your presentation the children should know:

⚜ That a quilt is composed of three layers held together by quilting stitches.
⚜ The difference between pieced and appliqué quilt blocks.
⚜ How to identify 4-patch, 9-patch, and 16-patch quilt blocks.
⚜ How long it takes to make a quilt.
⚜ That quilts are works of art and should be handled with care.
⚜ That quilts may be used on beds or hung on walls.

Try to show and display several quilts made from different designs and a variety of techniques. Bring at least one quilt the children may touch. If you don't have any quilts, use pictures in books or old quilt calendars (these

Children will have lots of questions and want to share their own stories about quilts.

may be laminated for longer life). Kindergartners (five and six year olds) stay attentive for about 15 minutes, so the quilt show should be simple. Fifth graders (ten and 11 year olds) will sit for 45 minutes, so expand the presentation to include more details about the quilts, their history, and their construction. Block patterns, secondary patterns, color use, three-dimensional illusions, overall design, and quilting patterns may all be discussed.

Pitch your presentation at the appropriate level. Allow time at the end for the children to ask questions and tell you about the quilts they have at home or have seen. The children love to participate, so ask them questions to encourage them to make observations about the quilts you show.

What Is a Quilt?

Ask the children, "What is a quilt?" Usually they answer, "It has patchwork," "It is a blanket," "It has patterns," "It has lots of colors," "It is warm." Explain how a quilt differs from a blanket or bed cover.

A quilt has three layers: a *top* that may be pieced with colored patches or whole-cloth; a *batting* (or wadding) made from cotton, polyester, or wool; and a *back*, usually of one fabric but which may be pieced. These three layers are like a sandwich stitched together with quilting stitches. The quilting stitches are a vital component. Tacked or tied bed covers are often called quilts, but they are actually comforters and not true quilts, since they have no quilting stitches.

Pass around a small piece, 12" (30 cm) square, of all three layers with some quilting stitches holding them together in the middle. Leave the sides unfinished so the children can feel the batting and see that the top, batting, and back make a sandwich. Tell them how much work goes into making a quilt, and that quilts should be handled with care and treated with respect.

During my work in 1997, some children observed that "Quilts are pieces of art." This surprised me, since in 1994, none of the children mentioned it. I think this reflects the gradual education of nonquilters and the acceptance of quilts as works of art by other artists and the public.

Maggie showing Wendy's sampler, where the blocks are all of different patterns.

Types of Quilts

Explain that many quilts are constructed from blocks. The most common block shape is a square, and the pattern is often repeated. Show the children a quilt, or a picture of a quilt, with square blocks. The blocks may be set next to one another squarely, or on the point, and may have sashing strips between them. Encourage the children to discuss the patterns and colors.

Describe the difference between pieced and appliqué blocks and show examples. In pieced blocks, the patchwork shapes are cut out and stitched together. In appliqué, a background block is cut and the pieces are usually sewn onto it by either turning the edges under and blind stitching them down by hand, or by satin stitching the raw edge with a sewing machine.

Quilts where the blocks are all of different patterns are called samplers. Showing a sampler quilt is an excellent way to introduce several block designs (see *Color Wheel Sampler* page 103).

The children can identify the most common shapes used within the blocks (squares, triangles, diamonds). Explain the way square pieced blocks may be divided into smaller, often repeating, units. They are usually 4-patch, 9-patch, or 16-patch blocks made from four, nine, or 16 units respectively. The units may be subdivided into smaller squares, triangles, or rectangles to create different patterns.

4-patch

Two blocks of the same pattern may appear very different because of the colors used or the placement of the direction of a striped fabric. Older children will be interested to learn that the pioneers, recycling scraps of clothing and odd pieces of cloth, made and named quilt blocks after their surroundings, e.g., Bear Paw, Turkey Tracks, Rocky Road to Kansas, Ohio Star, Snowflake, Log Cabin, Maple Leaf, and Mariner's Compass. Some blocks have more than one name and/or local variations in design.

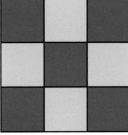

9-patch

The Log Cabin is a good block to discuss. Tell the children that traditionally the strips represented the logs of the cabin and the center was red to signify the fire or hearth in the

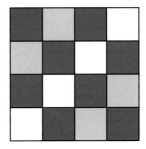

16-patch

home, or yellow for the lantern in the window. Show how Log Cabin blocks usually have dark logs on two sides and light logs on the other two sides.

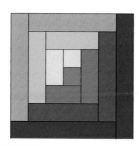

Basic Log Cabin block.

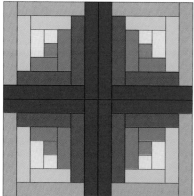

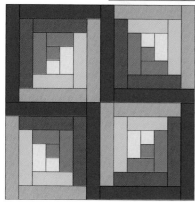

Four different settings for the Log Cabin block.

Blocks are not always square. We showed a Sugar Loaf quilt made up of triangles (ask the children to identify the block shape). The Sugar Loaf design is so-called because sugar used to be sold in compressed triangular cones, and pieces were chipped away as they were needed.

The Sunbow Star quilt is one giant block made up of many diamonds. This design is also called the Texas Lone Star or the Star of Bethlehem. Large triangles and squares are set between the points of the star to square it off. These large plain areas are ideal for fancy quilting designs.

Maggie showing Wendy's Sunbow Star *quilt.*

If possible, show an example of an antique quilt. I have a small Victorian Tumbling Blocks couch throw. The Tumbling Block is made up of three equally sized diamonds. Ask the children what the design looks like and see if they can tell you that the three-dimensional effect is created by the way dark and light fabrics are used. At this stage in the presentation you could also talk about Victorian crazy quilts and their fine embroidery stitches.

Quilts With Secondary Patterns

Kaleidoscope quilts are made up of identical blocks, but, because of the color use and the shape of the pieces, a larger design is created that extends beyond the boundary of the basic block. Within the block there are eight large triangles and four smaller ones in the corners. There

Kaleidoscopic Garden *shows how the color and the shape of the pieces can create a larger design.*

are no curved pieces, but a secondary design of circles emerges.

In the quilt *Kaleidoscopic Garden* the kaleidoscope principle is used. There are only two kinds of blocks in the quilt but the color placement gives the quilt one large overall design. The circles of flowers are appliquéd and the rest of the patchwork is machine pieced. The children were able to pick out the small 9-patches and see the large circles created by the kaleidoscopic effect. Distinguishing the boundaries of the two different alternating blocks was difficult for them.

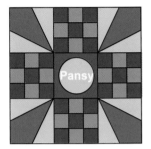 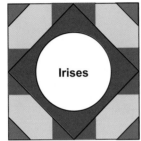

The two basic blocks in the *Kaleidoscope Garden* quilt.

The kaleidoscope principle

Quilting

If possible, bring a half-quilted quilt so the children can see the difference between the quilted areas and those yet to be stitched. Show them the basting stitches and explain that these are temporary and hold the three layers of the quilt together until the quilting is complete. Show them how the quilting design is marked on the quilt, and point out variations in design such as crosshatch, wreath, feather, quilting in the ditch, and quilting 1/4" from the seam lines. The quilting pattern is an integral part of the overall design and can greatly enhance the appearance of the quilt.

Tell children how long it takes to do hand quilting. They are usually surprised to hear that it takes at least 150 to 200 hours to quilt a bed quilt, especially if you express it

Showing a half-quilted quilt.

in such terms as "an hour for every day you spend at school this year!" Some ornate quilts have over 700 hours of work in them. Show how quilting patterns stand out more clearly on solid colors, especially pale fabrics, than on busy patterned fabrics. Describe the action of quilting at a frame or show a hoop and demonstrate. You could mention quilting bees at this point. They will be awestruck at the small size of your quilting needle and the quilting stitches! Quilts may also be quilted by machine, which is much faster. If you have an example, demonstrate how the surface texture differs from hand quilting.

Wall Quilts

Not all quilts are designed for beds. Quilting is an art form and many quilters make wall hangings for display. Techniques such as embellishment with fancy threads, beads, and ribbon or three-dimensional work may not be durable enough for use on a bed, but are ideal for wall quilts.

This bear quilt is a wall hanging.

Fast Piecing Techniques

For children age ten and older, you can talk briefly about fast piecing techniques. Show the children a rotary cutter (rather like a pizza cutter). Tell the children that the blade of the rotary cutter is very sharp and that it should always be used with care. *Never put the rotary cutter down without the safety guard on the blade and do not allow the children unsupervised access.*

Explain how strip piecing can save time. For example, when making the small 9-patches in *Kaleidoscopic Garden*, three strips were sewn together and then cut to make lines of squares, instead of cutting out each individual square. Draw examples on the chalkboard - the children grasp the concept quickly.

+ + =

+ + =

Strip piecing 9-patches.

Strip piecing using 45° cuts to create diamonds.

Sharing Time

Allow time for questions and comments at the end of your presentation. Five to ten minutes should be sufficient. Some common questions we heard were: "How many quilts have you made?" "How long did it take you to make that quilt?" Which quilt do you use on your bed?" "Which is your favorite quilt?"

At one presentation I gave to first graders, after a few questions, time was running out so I said I would take one last question. I nodded to a little boy whose hand was raised and he asked, "Is it recess time?" Then I really knew my time was up!

Usually the children want to tell you things as well as ask questions. Often they have friends or relatives who quilt, or they have quilts at home. They enjoy sharing their experiences and should be encouraged to do so. They are usually extremely appreciative and you will receive rewarding compliments.

Research Topics

Older children may enjoy doing some research about different kinds of quilts and their historical origins.

Here are some suggestions for topics:

Amish quilts
Hawaiian quilts
Friendship and
    album quilts
Victorian crazy quilts
Quilted clothing
Civil War quilts
Dating antique quilts
Pictorial quilts
Quilting bees and
    traditions

Block designs, their
    names and origins
European quilts
Trapunto
Colonial quilts
African-American
    quilts
Broderie Perse and
    embroidered quilts

Add to or reduce your presentation as you feel appropriate for the audience. The best way to illustrate a point is to have a quilt or a picture for the children to see. This serves as an introduction to quilts and quilting. Your goal should be to communicate your enthusiasm and interest in the subject. Then the children will be eager to start their own quilting project.

"Thank you for all your hard work and effort for our class and school. I love your quilts! I will always keep sewing!"
                                        Lara, third grade

"I love quilting. I wish we could quilt every day."
                                        Katarina, age 9

Chapter Two

Teaching Children to Sew

Teaching children to sew is both challenging and rewarding. A key to success is giving the children as much individual attention as possible while they are mastering the basic skills. I recommend at least one adult per six children. With this level of supervision, the frustrations when the thread knots or breaks, or the needle comes unthreaded, are short lived. The children need to be repeatedly shown how to make the stitches, and they need help with starting and ending their sewing. The older the children, the better their fine motor skills, and the easier it is to teach them.

For groups, the children should be at least eight years old for hand sewing and ten years for machine sewing. Younger children can be taught to sew, but they require much more help and have a shorter attention span. Children age 11 or older can learn the skills easily and prepare their own materials. Boys are just as good at it as girls!

Warning! For classroom projects, keep all the work at school. If the children are allowed to take their work-in-progress home, some of it will disappear and will never come back to school!

TEACHING CHILDREN HAND SEWING

Introduce the children to some basic sewing terms. Show them the "right" (top) and the "wrong" (underside) side of the fabric. Explain that the way the fabric is woven gives it "grain" and show them the lengthwise grain, the cross grain, and the bias. Bias edges stretch and easily become misshapen, so patchwork pieces are usually cut with as many sides as possible aligned with the lengthwise or cross grain. The term straight grain refers to either the lengthwise or cross grains.

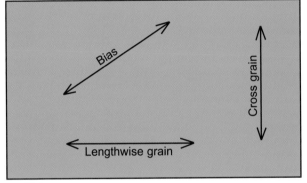

Selvage

Machine sewing a pillow back.

Learning to sew by hand takes concentration.

Use large-eyed needles (embroidery needles sizes 3 to 9). These are easy to thread and are a good size for small hands.

A convenient way for the children to store pins is in homemade pincushions. Before the first session, glue together two layers of 2" (5 cm) square Styrofoam (polystyrene) and add a square of denim to the top. These pincushions are about ⅜" (0.8 cm) thick and are large enough to store six to ten pins. The pins stick in easily and remain upright.

Basic Stitches for Patchwork

Begin by giving each child two strips of fabric (2" x 6", 5 x 15 cm works well), one dark and one light, for practicing the basic stitches. Demonstrate the following steps to the children, then supervise them closely while they do the stitching, helping them as they learn.

1. Draw the stitching line in pencil on the wrong side of the light strip of fabric. Use a ruler and make the line ¼" (0.75 cm) from the edge along one of the long sides of the strip.

2. Place the two strips right sides together so that the raw edges are aligned. Pin them together.

3. Cut a length of thread about 24" (60 cm) and thread the needle. Demonstrate by pinching the end of the thread between the thumb and first finger in one hand and holding the needle in the other hand. Bring the needle slowly towards the thread. A common mistake is to try to thread the needle with a large tail of thread hanging out of the thumb and first finger. The thread moves and it is difficult to insert into the eye of the needle. Pull the thread through the needle so the tails are of equal length. Knot the doubled thread once about 1" (2.5 cm) from the ends. Using doubled thread prevents the needle from coming unthreaded while the children are sewing, but mistakes are harder to undo. Older children, ten years or more, should be taught to sew with a single thread.

4. Right-handed children should hold the fabric pieces in their left hand with their thumb on top and their fingers beneath, and stitch from right to left. Left-handers will hold the fabric in their right hand, and stitch from left to right.

5. Take one running stitch on the marked seam line with

The correct hand position. My daughter, Hazel, stitches her pinned patches.

the knot on the top side. Always keep the side with the seam marking on the top. Take one backstitch. Demonstrate the backstitch to the children and tell them they're "doing the stitch over again."

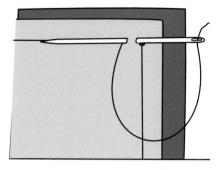

The backstitch. Tell the children to "do the stitch over again."

6. Take three running stitches, then a backstitch. This will give the stitches a little more strength and prevent them from gathering if the thread is pulled too tightly. Remind the children to always hold the fabric with the marked seam line on the top and work from this side. At first, they tend to turn the work over and get confused.

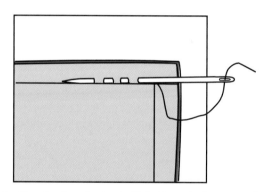

Start with a knot and a backstitch, then do three running stitches. Repeat until the seam is sewn.

7. Continue sewing with three running stitches followed by a backstitch until the seam is complete, or the thread is only 4" to 5" (10 to 12 cm) long. Make sure the children stop sewing before the thread becomes too short to end off.

8. To end off, take a tiny backstitch, slipping the needle through the loop as you pull it through. Repeat. Remove the pins.

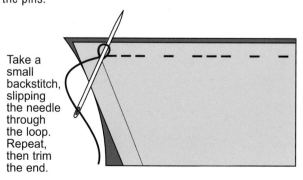

Take a small backstitch, slipping the needle through the loop. Repeat, then trim the end.

Once the children have completed a seam on their practice pieces, they are ready to start the quilt project.

Preparing Block Packets and Teaching How to Piece Quilt Blocks

There are several steps involved in making traditional quilt blocks. The preparation is time-consuming because all the pieces must be marked with stitching lines. This takes 15 to 30 minutes per block, depending on the number of patches. Find some volunteers to help you and have a work party to prepare the block packages.

Children 11 years or older can draw around the templates and cut their own patchwork pieces with your guidance. I recommend that you trace and cut out the plastic templates for the children (use template plastic marked with a ¼" or metric grid) to ensure that the correct shapes are used and that the sizes are accurate. Use the block diagrams, templates, and piecing instructions in Appendices 1 to 6 for making 9" (24 cm) blocks. If you want to make different size blocks, you will need to draft your own templates, but you may still use the piecing instructions.

1. Choose a block pattern from Appendix 1. You may want to reduce the choice to seven or eight blocks to simplify the project and use fewer templates.

2. Trace the inner dotted lines on the template diagrams in Appendix 6, and cut plastic templates for the block pieces. Appendix 2 tells you which templates are needed for each block.

3. Iron the fabric. Put a piece of fine sandpaper under it to prevent it from slipping while you draw around the templates. Place the templates on the wrong side of the fabric so that the maximum number of edges are parallel with the straight grain.

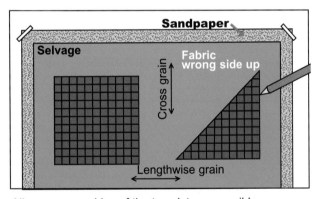

Align as many sides of the template as possible with the straight grain.

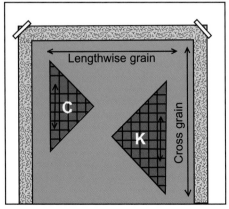

In Triangles C and K, only the long sides are on the straight grain and the two sides are on the bias. These are exceptions to the rule.

4. Draw around the templates with a lead or chalk pencil. These are the stitching lines. The outside edges of the assembled block should be on the straight grain. Bias edges stretch and easily go out of shape, so it is important to position the template with this is mind. Squares and rectangles may be placed squarely on the grain of the fabric. For right-angled triangles, the only bias edge should be the longest side (Triangles C and K are exceptions, where the long side should be on the straight grain and the other two sides on the bias). Many of the blocks use the same template shapes, so you will save time by marking all those of one shape before cutting.

5. Cut out the shapes, adding approximately ¼" (0.75 cm) seam allowance around all sides. Do not cut along the lines!

6. Check that you have the correct number of pieces and that they are the right shapes!

7. Store the pieces for each block in a zipper top plastic bag, along with a needle and a diagram of the block. Now the packages are ready for the children to begin sewing. Label them with the children's names.

8. The children should pin the block pieces, right side up, in the correct layout on a piece of paper (approx. 15", 35 cm square). Ask them to write their name and the name of the block on the paper.

9. Explain the piecing order to the children. This is important. If you follow the guides in Appendices 3 to 5, all the piecing will be in straight lines with no insetting of corners. As a general principle, piece the square units first, then sew these together in rows, and finish by joining the rows. For example, Shoo Fly, Contrary Wife, Wings in a Whirl, and Friendship Star are all 9-patches that have four of the nine square units divided into two half-square triangles. The triangles should be sewn together first to form squares, and then the squares sewn in rows of three. Next the rows are joined to complete the blocks.

10. Remove from the paper the first two pieces to be stitched.

11. Show the children the seam line markings and explain that these are the stitching lines, then teach them how to pin two pieces for sewing. Place the pieces right sides together and pin along the seam line. The pins should be perpendicular to the stitching line and all pointing the same way. Pin the ends first. Poke the pin through precisely at the marked corner on the top piece of fabric, then turn the two pieces over to make sure the point comes through on the corner marked on the second piece. Do the same for the other end of the stitching line. Align the pins

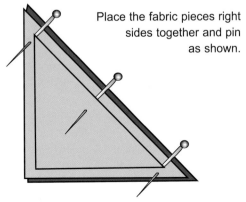

Place the fabric pieces right sides together and pin as shown.

at right angles to the marked line. When the ends are accurately pinned, pin the center. Check the back to make sure the pin is on the seam line. Add more pins if the seam is longer than 5" (12 cm) or if it has a bias edge. Accurate pinning takes a little time but will prevent problems later, so check it before the children start sewing.

12. Once the pinning is complete, the seams can be hand stitched. Use basic running and backstitches (take three running stitches, then a backstitch). Start with the needle ¼" (0.75 cm) away from the corner on the stitching line and bring it up precisely in the corner by the pin. Do a backstitch. The thread should come up in the corner. Sew with small running and backstitches along the seam line. Sew right into the corner, but not beyond the pencil line. Turn around and come back about ¼" (0.75 cm), then end off.

```
←   ←   ←   ←   ←   ←   ←   ←   ←
↱  End off                      Start ↰
```

The arrows indicate sewing direction (for right-handers). Start ¼" from the corner, backstitch into the corner, sew along the seam to the other corner, backstitch ¼" in, and end off.

13. Finger press the seam, pressing both parts of the seam allowance toward the side with the darker fabric.

14. Pin the stitched piece back onto the paper. Give the children an ultimatum! Make them keep all the patchwork pieces pinned on the paper, except for the two pieces being sewn. Pin finished sections back onto the paper in the correct position. This will prevent patchwork pieces from becoming lost and the children will be able to see how their blocks are progressing.

15. Continue stitching until the block is complete. When sewing two pieced patchwork sections together, it is often necessary to sew through a seam allowance. Do not sew over the seam allowance, but pass the needle through it next to the stitching line. This allows the seam allowance to be flipped in either direction. Make a backstitch on each side of the seam to ensure a strong join. In blocks such as the Old Windmill, eight seams meet in the middle. The children will probably need some extra help in the center of their final stitching line, which will be along the middle of the block (sewing the two halves together). When so many seams meet in one place, it is easy to lose the stitching line and end up with a hole or a poofy part in the middle.

16. When the block is complete, iron it with the seams toward the darker fabric, or in the direction they naturally fall. Where several seams come together, open them up so they don't all lay the same way and form a lump.

These blocks are challenging. Congratulate the children when their blocks are completed and show the work to everyone else. The children will be proud of their achievement. Obviously, some children will work faster than others. Encourage those who finish quickly to help others or to make another block if you have the materials prepared.

Appliqué

Traditionally, appliqué pieces are blind stitched onto a background fabric, using the needle to turn under a seam allowance of approximately ⅛". This is difficult for children, but there are other methods.

Helios Searches for the Perfect Stem was hand appliquéd by Maggie in 1996. It includes three-dimensional ruched stems and hand and machine quilting. The dragonfly is a finger puppet from the Seattle Art Museum.

Appliqué Using Fusible Webbing

Adhesive webbing (Steam-a-Seam 2, Wonder-Under), bonded by heat, can be used to appliqué a piece to a background. The appliqué piece should be cut to the finished size since the edge is not turned under. Where the pieces overlap, allow a little extra fabric. The edges may be overstitched by machine or hand stitched. This will add to the durability of the quilt, especially if it is to be used and washed repeatedly. Outlining with blanket stitching in colored embroidery floss looks attractive and works well since the needle passes through just one fused piece on each stitch. Don't ask the children to hand stitch through multiple fused layers, since pushing the needle through is too difficult

Appliqué Using Fusible Interfacing

The interfacing method for appliqué provides a way to turn under edges effectively and accurately. Use lightweight fusible interfacing and draw or trace the appliqué shape onto the nonadhesive side. Lay the interfacing, with the drawing on the top, on the right side of the fabric. Machine stitch along the line all the way around the shape. Cut it out, leaving a seam allowance no larger than ¼" (0.75 cm) and cut notches into the curves. Make a slit in the interfacing in the middle and turn it inside out. Now the right side of the fabric will be exposed and the adhesive side of the interfacing will be on the outside. Place the piece on the background and iron to fuse (follow the manufacturer's directions). Using this technique, the appliqué piece is firmly tethered and will not move around while the children sew. Use this method for the Sunbonnet Sue and heart appliqué blocks (Appendix 1 and Appendix 6).

Teach the children to sew with a hem or blind stitch in a thread color that matches the appliqué piece (rather than the color of the background). Alternatively, use a decorative embroidery stitch such as the blanket stitch in colored embroidery floss.

Sunbonnet Sue block steps for appliqué using fusible interfacing.

For Sunbonnet Sue, some of the pieces overlap, so care must be taken to fuse the pieces in the correct order. Cut a 10" (27 cm) square from a pale-colored fabric for the background. Select two calico prints, one for the dress and one for the bonnet, boots, and arm. Use plain cream, pale pink, or brown for the hand. Follow the steps described above but leave the jagged template lines unstitched. Note that the open edge of the boot goes under the dress, the bonnet goes over the top of the dress, and the open end of the hand goes under the arm. You may adjust the position of the arm and hand, and embroider, for example, a posy of flowers. When the sewing is completed, trim the block to 9½" (25.5 cm) square. Sunbonnet Sue blocks are time-consuming to prepare (approximately 30 minutes each), but are very popular with the children.

Embroidery

Children love to embroider. They learn the stitches quickly, especially if they have already learned the basic running and backstitch used in hand piecing. They enjoy selecting embroidery floss to add more color to their work and are eager to learn a variety of stitches.

Wind the embroidery floss onto cardboard to reduce waste. Skeins will rapidly become tangled into something resembling a bird's nest if the children are allowed to help themselves! The cardboard keeps the threads tidier and it is easier for the children to cut their own pieces.

Most embroidery floss is six stranded. I advise sewing with just three strands. Start by teaching the children how to divide the strands. Cut the floss about 18" (45 cm) long. Children should work in pairs. The child dividing the floss holds it up from one end, allowing it to dangle down. The second child holds their lightly clenched fist in a vertical position about 3" (8 cm) lower, with the thread passing through. The floss should be divided slowly. As the strands are separated, the dangling end rotates and the fist prevents tangling. A tightly clenched fist will not allow the floss to move. Make sure you demonstrate the correct way so the children understand. You will probably have to remind them at the start of each new session.

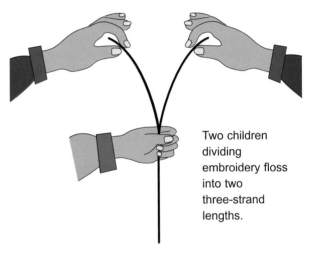

Two children dividing embroidery floss into two three-strand lengths.

Use a small piece of burlap or canvas, a large tapestry needle, and colored yarn or embroidery floss to demonstrate the stitches to a group of children. Knot the yarn or floss at one end and thread the other end through the needle. Teach one embroidery stitch at a time. We always began with the blanket stitch. Bring the thread from the back to the front so the knot remains on the back. Work the stitches on the front, and discourage the children from turning the sewing over, except to start and end. The floss should be tied off on the back. Children tend to sew until their thread is too short to tie off. They also forget to move

M.J. demonstrates the blanket stitch.

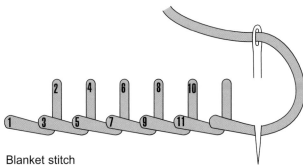

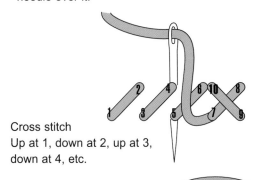

Blanket stitch
Up at 1, down at 2, hold the thread down and bring the needle over it.

Cross stitch
Up at 1, down at 2, up at 3, down at 4, etc.

Chain stitch
Up at 1, down at 2, hold the loop in place close to the fabric, up at 3, down at 4, etc.

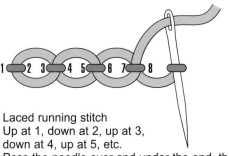

Laced running stitch
Up at 1, down at 2, up at 3, down at 4, up at 5, etc.
Pass the needle over and under the end, then switch directions and complete the loops as shown.

the needle up the floss as the floss is used, causing the tail to be caught in their sewing. Sometimes they pull the floss too tight, creating puckers. Watch for these errors and give the children as much individual attention as possible. Once they master the blanket stitch, the other stitches will be easy. Our children blanket stitched around heart shapes before starting on the chain stitch, cross stitch, and laced running stitch.

If you have metallic gold or silver embroidery floss, the children will be itching to use it. It tends to fray easily when it is pulled through the fabric for the traditional stitches. In the laced running stitch, it may be passed in and out of a running stitch on the surface. This will add a little sparkle, which the children love, without the fraying and tangling problems.

TEACHING CHILDREN MACHINE SEWING

Children 11 years or older usually have the motor skills and level of maturity necessary to use a sewing machine. Of course, this is not a hard and fast rule. There are some extremely capable nine-year-olds and some very uncoordinated 15-year-olds! Use your discretion. If the child shows an interest and has the motivation of an enjoyable project, you will have fun and be successful. Children may be apprehensive about using a sewing machine, but their initial hesitation is soon dispelled when they sit down and see that it is not difficult to operate, and it sews neatly and fast! Make sure your sewing machine is in good working order.

Practicing sewing on graph paper.

Show the children how a sewing machine operates and how it is threaded. Start them sewing on a piece of graph paper with no thread in the machine. The needle will punch holes in the paper and the children will become familiar with the feel of the machine. Their confidence and control of the motor action will increase and they will be able to see whether they are sewing in a straight line. Trim the edge of a piece of graph paper along one of the marked lines, then the stitching line can be sewn a measured distance from the edge of the paper (the seam allowance). Have them practice sewing with an accurate ¼" (0.75 cm) seam allowance by placing a narrow piece of masking tape on the machine bed next to the edge of the graph paper when the needle is exactly positioned for the ¼" (0.75 cm) seam allowance. If the raw edges of the fabric pieces are positioned and fed through the machine adjacent to the edge of the masking tape, the ¼" (0.75 cm) seam allowance will be maintained. Some sewing machines have a ¼" foot or markings on the plate, in which case it is not necessary to use the masking tape.

Assembly-line machine sewing Log Cabin blocks.

Teach the children to assembly-line sew, feeding the pieces through the machine one after another, and using a scrap of fabric as a spacer when they finish each batch of sewing. This saves time and enables them to start stitching at the edge of the fabric without the thread knotting or the fabric gathering. You will be surprised how quickly their confidence increases and how much they enjoy using the machine.

When machine piecing, it is not necessary to mark the stitching lines on the fabric. Just use a consistent ¼" (0.75 cm) seam allowance. The fabric should be cut ¼" (0.75 cm) larger on each side than the desired finished size. For example, for a finished border strip 2" x 45" (5 x 115 cm), cut the strip 2½" x 45½" (6.5 x 116.5 cm). If templates are used, they should include the seam allowance (this is different from hand sewing where the template size is the same as the finished size). See Appendix 6 for templates that include the seam allowance for machine piecing traditional quilt blocks. Use the outer solid line on the template diagrams. See Appendices 1 to 6 for block diagrams and piecing instructions.

Show the children how to butt seam allowances (see page 31 for instructions) and teach them how to press their patchwork with both seam allowances toward the darker fabric.

A simple project like a small doll quilt made from a variety of 4" (10 cm) squares is a good way to introduce the children to the sewing machine and practice an accurate ¼" (0.75 cm) seam allowance. After this you will easily be able to move on to more complicated projects involving several sizes of pieces and different geometric shapes such as those used in traditional quilt blocks.

TEACHING CHILDREN HAND QUILTING

Hand quilting is time-consuming but the children love it. They are content to sit in small groups around a quilting frame - their own little quilting bee - chatting while they work. Make sure every child in the group has the opportunity to try. You will have trouble tearing some of them away from the quilt frame, and you may have to set time limits to make sure everyone has a turn. "I love quilting," "I wish we could do quilting every day," were comments that greeted me as I set up the quilt frame for each quilting session at school. They made my day.

Showing how to do hand quilting on a frame.

Children working on individual projects should use a 14" embroidery hoop for quilting. Don't give them larger hoops because their hands won't be able to reach the center underneath.

Hand quilting around a heart.

Quilting with an embroidery hoop.

Before quilting begins, the three layers of the quilt sandwich must be basted together (see page 32 for instructions). Show the children a half-quilted quilt, with basting stitches and marks for the quilting lines. They will see the difference between the area that has already been quilted and that part not yet stitched. On the children's quilts, keep the quilting designs simple. Here are some suggestions that require no markings:

1. Quilt around the edge of each block, in or near the ditch (avoid quilting through the seam allowance).
2. Use masking tape as a guide to quilt ¼" away from the seams on geometric patterns.
3. Quilt 9-patch squares with diagonal lines from corner to corner (use strips of masking tape for stitching guides).
4. Quilt around the outside of shapes like hearts and Sunbonnet Sue.

If you need to mark the quilt, use a fine lead pencil (Ultimate Marking Pencil for Quilters), a Berol silver pencil, or chalk pencils. You may like to machine quilt around each block "in the ditch" then allow the children to hand quilt inside the blocks. This helps stabilize the quilt during the hand quilting, and less hand quilting is necessary.

Quilting needles are small for children to handle and thread. Use size 7. The children will probably need help threading the needle at first. Make sure you have a selection of different sized thimbles available. Demonstrate hand quilting to them in a hoop or on a frame, showing them the following steps.

1. Thread the needle with a piece of quilting thread approximately 18" (45 cm) long and make a knot close to the end. You may use beeswax on the thread (optional) to help smooth stitching and reduce tangling.

2. Bury the knot in the batting by inserting the needle into the middle layer about 1½" (4 cm) from the starting point. Move it through the batting, bringing it to the surface at the starting point. Pull the thread until the knot and tail pop through the top of the quilt and disappear into the batting.

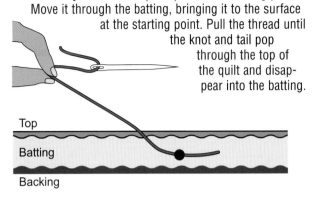

Top

Batting

Backing

3. Move the needle with a rocking motion, stitching through all three layers of the quilt.

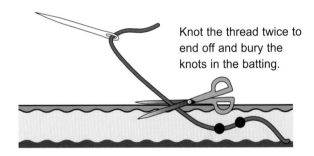

Stitch through all three layers.

4. End off by knotting the thread twice within 1" (2.5 cm) of the quilt surface, and burying the knots in the batting as you did at the start.

Knot the thread twice to end off and bury the knots in the batting.

The children will find using a thimble awkward when they start. They must work from the top of the quilt, with the needle in one hand and the other hand under the quilt to push the needle up as it comes through to the back of the quilt. There is a tendency to flip over work in a hoop, or creep under the quilt frame to catch the needle underneath! The first stitch is the most difficult. The point of the needle must be pushed up from below with the index finger as soon as it penetrates the back. Then the thimble should be used to push the needle as it moves up and down through the quilt. You will be surprised how quickly most of the children learn the rocking motion. Tell them to take two or three stitches at a time, but no more. For some children this is difficult, so they may need to take just one stitch at a time.

Children working on individual projects will soon become proficient at starting and ending their threads. If you are working with 30 children on one quilt, each child will spend a relatively small amount of time quilting and they will need help with threading needles and starting and stopping. Work with small groups of three or four children around a medium-sized frame and up to six on a large quilting frame. The more experienced quilters you have to help the children, the easier it will be.

We made our own medium-sized quilting frame from 60" long 1" x 2" planks wrapped in muslin and clamped in the corners with C-clamps. This was flat and could be conveniently stored against a wall in the classroom.

Tying

Tying is a fast way to finish a quilt and the children may easily participate in tying the knots. Technically, a tied quilt is really a comforter (quilts must have quilting stitches). Quilts to be tied may be basted with safety pins. Use embroidery floss or pearl cotton in a color or variety of colors that complement the quilt top.

Maggie and volunteers pin a quilt onto the frame.

1. Mark the positions for the ties, spacing them evenly no more than 6" (15 cm) apart.

2. Using a large needle, take a small stitch through all the layers at the position for the tie. Pull the thread through and leave a tail of 3" to 4" (8 to 10 cm). Move to the next tying point and take a small stitch through all the layers. Continue in this way, threading the needle again as necessary. Cut the threads midway between the tying points.

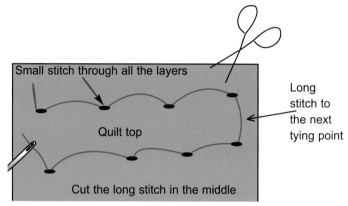

Stitch the ties using long threads.

3. Use the tails to firmly tie square knots over the stitches (right over left and under, then left over right and under). The children may work in pairs, one placing a finger over a half knot to prevent it from loosening while the other completes the knot. Check the children's knots to make sure they are secure and tight.

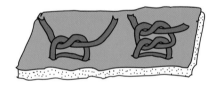

Use the tails to tie square knots.

4. Trim the tails to the desired length.

Chapter Three
Quilting Basics

Do you need help estimating the quantity of fabric you will need for your project, rotary cutting, arranging the blocks, choosing appropriate fabrics for sashing and borders, assembling, quilting, and finishing your quilt? These standard techniques are outlined below. More detailed descriptions of these and other techniques may be found in such useful books as *Quilter's Complete Guide* by Marianne Fons and Liz Porter, *Marsha McCloskey's Guide to Rotary Cutting,* and *Machine Quilting Made Easy!* by Maurine Noble.

ESTIMATING YARDAGE

Most 100% cotton "quilting" fabrics measure 42" to 44" (106 to 112 cm) wide. This is the size used in my estimates below. Some fabrics are narrower (36", 90 cm) and some are wider (60", 150 cm), so adjust your estimates accordingly.

How many units will you need? Allow some extras for errors or lost work. How big are the units? These may be blocks, large panels, strips, whole-cloth, or a combination. Remember to include the seam allowances (¼", 0.75 cm) on each side.

For group quilts, I usually wait until the children's work is completed and I've figured out the exact quilt layout before determining the sashing and border fabric requirements. Draw a sketch of your quilt on graph paper and count the number of sashing and border strips. Now itemize your fabric needs.

- How many and what size are the frames around the blocks?
- How many and what size are the sashing strips?
- How many and what size are the squares of a different fabric at the sashing intersections?
- How many and what size are the outer borders?
- What size is the backing?
- What size is the binding?

Follow the guidelines below and use the tables on pages 27-27 to help you calculate fabric requirements. Round up to the nearest ¼ yard/meter of fabric and if in doubt, allow a little extra. It is most frustrating to run out of a vital piece just before completing a project. Do not use the selvages.

1. How many units (blocks, sashing strips, borders etc.) will fit across one width of fabric? Divide the width of the fabric by the length or width of the unit.
2. How many cuts across the width of the fabric are needed to make all the units? Divide the total number of units by the answer to question 1.
3. How wide are the cuts?
4. How much fabric is needed? Multiply the answers of question 2 and 3 together.

Example 1:
Fabric needed for 28 blocks, 6½" square (25 children + 3 extras)

1. 42" ÷ 6½" = 6 blocks will fit across 1 fabric width.
2. 28 ÷ 6 = 5 widths will be required to make all the blocks.
3. These widths will be cut 6½" wide.
4. 5 widths x 6½" = 32½" of fabric. Round up = 1 yard needed.

Example 2:
Fabric needed to cut 20 rectangular blocks, 5½" x 8" (18 children + 2 extras)

1. 42" ÷ 5½" or 8" - see which is the most economical use of the fabric. 5½" = 7 times with a remainder of 3½" 8" = 5 times with a remainder of 2" Use 8"
2. 20 ÷ 5 = 4 widths will be required to make all the blocks.
3. These widths will be cut 5½" wide, then counter-cut 8".
4. 4 widths x 5½" wide = 22" of fabric. Round up = ¾ yard needed.

FABRIC REQUIREMENTS IN INCHES FOR A VARIETY OF SIZES AND NUMBERS OF BLOCKS

Cut strips across the full width of the fabric, then counter-cut the strips to make the blocks. This table is for fabric 42" wide.

Round the figures up to the next ¼ yard to allow for errors and straightening raw edges.

9" = ¼ yard	54" = 1½ yards	99" = 2¾ yards
18" = ½ yard	63" = 1¾ yards	108" = 3 yards
27" = ¾ yard	72" = 2 yards	126" = 3½ yards
36" = 1 yard	81" = 2¼ yards	
45" = 1¼ yards	90" = 2½ yards	

Size of Block (inches)	Number of Blocks						Notes
	5	**10**	**15**	**20**	**25**	**30**	
5 x 5	5	10	10	15	20	20	
5½ x 5½	5½	11	16½	16½	22	27½	
6 x 6	6	12	18	18	24	30	
6½ x 6½	6½	13	19½	26	32½	32½	
7 x 7	7	14	21	28	35	35	
7½ x 7½	7½	15	22½	30	37½	45	
8 x 8	8	16	24	32	40	48	
8½ x 8½	17	25½	34	42½	59½	68	
9 x 9	18	27	36	45	63	72	
9½ x 9½	19	28½	38	47½	66½	76	
10 x 10	20	30	40	50	70	80	
10½ x 10½	21	31½	42	52½	73½	84	
11 x 11	22	44	55	77	99	110	
11½ x 11½	23	46	57½	80½	103½	115	
12 x 12	24	48	60	84	108	120	
12½ x 12½	25	50	62½	87½	112½	125	
3½ x 5½	5½	5½	11	11	16½	16½	Cut strips 5½"
4 x 6	6	6	12	12	18	18	Cut strips 6"
4½ x 6½	6½	13	13	19½	19½	26	Cut strips 6½"
4½ x 8½	8½	17	17	25½	25½	34	Cut strips 8½"
5 x 7	5	10	15	20	25	25	Cut strips 5"
5½ x 8	5½	11	16½	22	27½	33	Cut strips 5½"
6½ x 8½	8 ½	17	25½	34	42½	42½	Cut strips 8½"
8 x 10	10	20	30	40	50	60	Cut strips 10"

FABRIC REQUIREMENTS IN CENTIMETERS FOR A VARIETY OF SIZES AND NUMBERS OF BLOCKS

Cut strips across the full width of the fabric, then counter-cut the strips to make the blocks.

This table is for fabric 106 cm wide. Round these figures up to the next quarter (0.25) meter to allow for errors and straightening raw edges.

25 cm = 0.25 meter	150 cm = 1.5 meters
50 cm = 0.5 meter	175 cm = 1.75 meters
75 cm = 0.75 meter	200 cm = 2 meters
100 cm = 1 meter	250 cm = 2.5 meters
125 cm = 1.25 meters	300 cm = 3 meters

Size of Block (centimeters)	Number of Blocks						Notes
	5	10	15	20	25	30	
12 x 12	12	24	24	36	48	48	
13.5 x 13.5	13.5	27	40.5	40.5	54	67.5	
15 x 15	15	30	45	45	60	75	
16.5 x 16.5	16.5	33	49.5	66	82.5	82.5	
18 x 18	18	36	54	72	90	108	
19.5 x 19.5	19.5	39	58.5	78	97.5	117	
21 x 21	21	42	63	84	105	126	
22.5 x 22.5	45	67.5	90	112.5	157.5	180	
24 x 24	48	72	96	120	168	192	
25 x 25	50	75	100	125	175	200	
26.5 x 26.5	53	79.5	106	132.5	185.5	212	
28 x 28	56	112	140	196	252	280	
30 x 30	60	120	150	210	270	300	
32 x 32	64	128	160	224	288	320	
33 x 33	66	132	165	231	297	330	
9.5 x 13.5	13.5	13.5	27	27	40.5	40.5	Cut strips 13.5 cm
10 x 15	15	15	30	30	45	45	Cut strips 15 cm
11.5 x 16.5	11.5	23	34.5	46	57.5	57.5	Cut strips 11.5 cm
11.5 x 21	11.5	23	34.5	46	57.5	69	Cut strips 11.5 cm
12 x 18	12	24	36	48	60	72	Cut strips 12 cm
13.5 x 20	13.5	27	40.5	54	67.5	81	Cut strips 13.5 cm
16.5 x 21	16.5	33	49.5	66	82.5	99	Cut strips 16.5 cm
20 x 24	24	48	72	96	120	144	Cut strips 24 cm

Often border strips are longer than one width of fabric (42", 106 cm). To make a border with no joins, you will use more fabric. For example, a quilt top 60" long with the border cut lengthwise on the fabric will require nearly 1¾ yards. For many fabrics, a join is scarcely visible, and you will need far less fabric. Alternatively, consider a pieced border using more than one fabric.

For quilts with straight edges, the binding may be cut on the straight grain of the fabric. I make my bindings from 2½" (7 cm) wide strips, cutting the ends at 45°, then joining the strips. To calculate how many strips to cut, measure the perimeter of the quilt and divide by 40 (100 for metric). For example, the average size of a classroom quilt is about 50" x 60" (125 x 150 cm) so the perimeter is 220" (550 cm). Divide this by 40" (100 cm). Six strips are needed at 2½" (7 cm). A total of 15" (42 cm) is required, so allow ½ yard (½ meter). Instead of binding, you may decide to bring the back of the quilt around to the front. This saves fabric but the edge of the quilt will not be so robust.

The batting and back of the quilt should be a minimum of 1½" (4 cm) larger on each side than the quilt top. For example, for a quilt top 42" x 64" (106 x 164 cm), make the back and cut the batting at least 45" x 67" (114 x 172 cm). Quilt backs may be pieced down the middle or by adding side strips, or any way you desire. If the quilt is to be hand quilted, try to keep the number of seams to a minimum because they are hard to stitch. For machine quilting, this is not a problem.

ROTARY CUTTING

Rotary cutters are wonderful timesaving cutting tools. Accurately sized pieces of fabric may be cut quickly in multiple layers. I cannot imagine precisely cutting 30 blocks with scissors, using a pencil to mark the cutting lines! This task can be done in less than 15 minutes with a rotary cutter, a cutting board, and a large ruler. I recommend Olfa rotary cutters (minimum size 45 mm), Olfa mats (minimum size 17" x 23", 43 x 60 cm), and Omnigrid rulers (6" x 24", and 15" square, 15 x 60 cm, and 31.5 cm square). The 15" square is not essential but is extremely useful for cutting blocks larger than 6" square. If you are unfamiliar with these tools, seek the help of a quilter or ask at your local quilt store for a demonstration.

Understand that you must never allow the rotary cutter to leave your hand with the blade exposed. I cannot emphasize this enough. Always use the safety catch, even if you are going to immediately pick up the cutter again to make another cut (who knows, you may be interrupted). Make a habit of closing the blade before you put it down.

1. Press the fabric.
2. Fold the fabric selvage to selvage. You may find that the raw edge has not been cut straight, but make the fold so that the fabric will lie flat.
3. Fold the fabric again in the same direction and place it flat on the cutting mat with the selvage edges at the top.
4. Cut to straighten the raw edge. Line up a horizontal line on your ruler with the fold at the bottom of the fabric. Move the ruler as close as possible to the raw edge of the fabric so there is a minimum of waste, but so that the raw edges on all the layers of fabric are exposed. Hold the ruler firmly in position with one hand. Hold the cutter as you would a sharp knife with your forefinger extended, and the shaft upright with the blade flush against the ruler. Apply some downward pressure and make the cut in one motion away from yourself, keeping the blade next to the edge of the ruler. Maintaining the position of the ruler, remove the raw edge you just cut. If your cut did not penetrate all the layers, repeat the cut with your ruler still in place. Now you have a straight edge!

Only older children should be allowed to use rotary cutters.

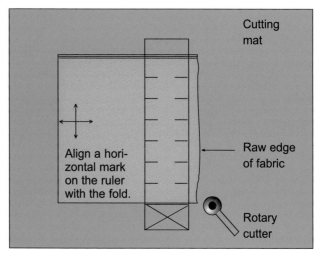

Cut to straighten the raw edge.

5. To make the next cut, either move around the table to the other side of the cutting board or carefully rotate the fabric without disturbing the straight edge. Cut strips the

desired width, using the ruler or square. If your original cut was not straight, or the ruler slipped on the second cut, you will have doglegs in the strip. Straighten the edge and try again!

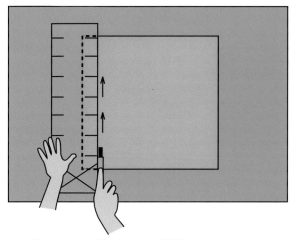

Cut the strips to the desired width.

6. Counter-cut strips to make blocks or pieces the desired size.

7. Don't forget to close the blade on the rotary cutter. The blade is very sharp!

Do not allow children unsupervised access to the rotary cutter. Children 11 years or older who behave responsibly may be taught how to use the cutter, but they still require strict supervision. A trip to the local hospital would really disrupt your quilting session! They might bleed on the fabric too! Joking aside, this wonderful time-saving device must be used with the utmost care.

CHOOSING SASHING AND BORDER FABRICS

Once the children have finished making the blocks, it is time to construct the quilt top. Choosing a suitable layout for the blocks and appropriate sashing and border fabrics will dramatically affect the appearance of the quilt. If the

Penguins on Parade *shows how the use of colorful sashing highlights the blocks.*

blocks are pale fabrics illustrated with fabric markers and crayons, brightly colored frames, sashing, and borders will enhance them and make them stand out. Time spent looking for the right fabrics is time well spent. Lay out the blocks with a variety of fabrics to see which looks best. If you don't have your own fabric stash, take the blocks to a fabric store and pull out several bolts of fabric to see how they look. You may be surprised by the colors that look great

Hot pink would not be the color that immediately comes to mind to frame these penguin blocks, but I auditioned several colors and rejected them. The pink made the blocks jump out and looks good with the blue snowflake sashing. Note the use of penguin fabric for the sashing corner squares.

Fabric choice is important and will make or break the quilt. You want the blocks to be clearly visible and enhanced. It is for this reason that I usually wait until the children's work is completed before I select the other fabrics, unless I already have a particularly appropriate theme fabric picked out. If you have already chosen a theme fabric or a multicolored print for the sashing, make sure the layout is not too busy. Consider framing the blocks with narrow strips of bright solid colors, which are wonderful for defining each block and brightening the appearance of the quilt.

Detail from Endangered Species *shows the use of a theme fabric.*

Close-ups from Happy Hilarious Animals *show the use of solid colors to frame the blocks and separate them from the jungle theme sashing strips.*

PIECING THE QUILT TOP

The piecing method that follows is the one most widely used. For a quilt made from blocks of all the same size, count the blocks and decide on the best configuration. Some numbers are extremely hard to format, so consider making additional blocks. A title block or blocks including the names of all the children are easy to add. You will find no shortage of volunteers to make the extra blocks. Use the table as a guide for possible piecing configurations.

Number of Blocks	Suggested Configurations
4	2 x 2
5	1 x 5, or make 1 more and use 6
6	2 x 3, 3 x 2
7	awkward number, make 1 or 2 more and use 8 or 9
8	2 x 4, 4 x 2
9	3 x 3
10	2 x 5, 5 x 2, or make 2 more and use 12
11	awkward number, make 1 more and use 12
12	2 x 6, 6 x 2, 3 x 4, 4 x 3
13	awkward number, make 2 or 3 more and use 15 or 16
14	2 x 7, 7 x 2, or make 1 or 2 more and use 15 or 16
15	3 x 5, 5 x 3
16	4 x 4, 2 x 8, 8 x 2
17	awkward number, make 1 or 3 more and use 18 or 20
18	3 x 6, 6 x 3, 2 x 9, 9 x 2
19	awkward number, make 1 more and use 20
20	4 x 5, 5 x 4, 2 x 10, 10 x 2
21	3 x 7, 7 x 3, or make 3 more and use 24
22	awkward number, make 2 or 3 more and use 24 or 25
23	awkward number, make 1 or 2 more and use 24 or 25
24	4 x 6, 6 x 4, 3 x 8, 8 x 3
25	5 x 5
26	awkward number, make 2 or 4 more and use 28 or 30
27	3 x 9, 9 x 3, or make 1 or 3 more and use 28 or 30
28	4 x 7, 7 x 4, or make 2 more and use 30
29	awkward number, make 1 more and use 30
30	5 x 6, 6 x 5, 3 x 10, 10 x 3

The blocks can be set side by side, but you may find that the designs merge together. Framing them and/or separating them with sashing strips creates a much bigger visual impact. Borders may be added around the outside edges.

For quilts with a large central panel surrounded by smaller blocks, space the blocks evenly or in a visually balanced format.

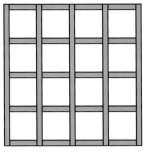

Blocks set squarely with sashing strips.

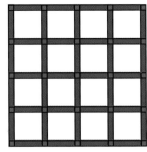

Blocks set squarely with sashing strips and corner squares.

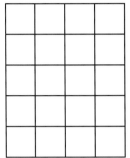

Blocks set squarely and adjacent.

Blocks set on-point and adjacent.

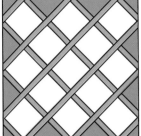

Blocks set on-point with sashing strips.

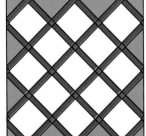

Blocks set on-point with sashing strips and corner squares.

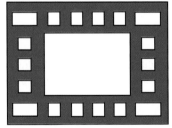

Large panel surrounded by smaller blocks.

1. Whatever your configuration, draw a sketch of the *finished* quilt top to scale on graph paper, including the block layout, sashing strips (with squares at the intersections if desired), and borders. Calculate the sizes (adding seam allowances) and the number of pieces you need to cut.

2. Press the fabric and rotary cut the pieces.

3. Machine stitch the quilt top together, sewing the blocks and sashing strips in rows, then joining the rows in long straight lines, so there are no inset corners. If each block is framed, sew the framing strips onto the blocks before adding the sashing strips. Assembly-line stitch, feeding pieces through the machine one after another.

4. Press the seams away from the blocks and toward the frames and sashings. For sashings with squares at the

intersections, press the seams away from the squares and toward the strips. Then the seam allowances will butt up snugly when the rows of pieces are joined, since they will have been pressed in opposite directions.

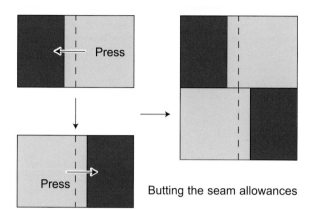

Butting the seam allowances

5. To add an outer border, measure the quilt top across the center from top to bottom. Cut the two side strips the same size and attach them to the quilt top. Press and measure the quilt top again, this time across the middle from side to side. Use this measurement for the top and bottom borders. Sometimes the edges of the quilt top become stretched and are larger than the middle. Make the border strips fit by easing in the extra fabric. If you use the edge measurement, the quilt top may have a wavy edge or may not lie flat. You can miter the corners if you like.

Quilts with different sized quilt blocks or rectangular blocks in both landscape and portrait format are a real challenge to piece. I advise using the appliqué technique described below unless you are experienced, enjoy math, and can draft patterns! For *Historic Bainbridge Island,* page 40, I laid the framed quilt blocks and central panel on top of the background fabric and arranged a satisfactory layout. Next I cut out scaled down graph paper blocks, squares for the written blocks, and rectangles for the pictorial blocks. I joined two pieces of graph paper together and drew the large central panel in the middle. I then positioned the paper squares and rectangles and taped them on the graph paper according to my layout. Next I labeled and calculated the sizes of the spaces between the blocks, added seam allowances, and double-checked all my calculations. This took me three hours and I hadn't even started cutting fabric and piecing! It really did tax my brain! If all the numbers are correct, the sewing is not difficult, but you need to plan the piecing order carefully to avoid insetting corners.

APPLIQUÉING QUILT BLOCKS ONTO A BACKGROUND

Adding frames to the blocks and appliquéing them onto a background is an easy way to cope with multiple sizes of blocks. The exact number of blocks is not important and will make no difference to the ease of construc-

tion. You may arrange the blocks any way you like on the background. Add extra blocks only if they are needed for balance or visual impact.

Make the frames for the blocks from strips of fabric folded in half and sew the two raw edges to the block so the fold is on the outer edge of the frame. Then stitch the folded edge to the background fabric by hand or machine.

This quilt was made with the appliqué piecing method.

For *Bainbridge Island Past and Present* (above), the colored frames surrounding the blocks measure $5/8$" wide. These were made from strips cut $1\frac{3}{4}$". To calculate the size of strip to cut, first decide how wide you would like the finished frame. Double this width and add two seam allowances.

For a 1" frame:
Cut the strips $2\frac{1}{2}$" wide
$(1 \times 2) + \frac{1}{4} + \frac{1}{4} = 2\frac{1}{2}$

For a 2 cm frame:
Cut the strips 5.5 cm wide
$(2 \times 2) + 0.75 + 0.75 = 5.5$

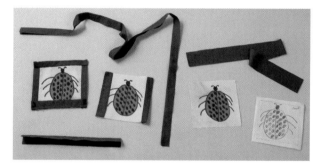

Adding framing strips to blocks for appliqué.

1. Calculate the width of strip to cut for the frames.
2. Cut the strips, fold them in half lengthwise, and press.
3. Cut two folded strips the same length as two sides of each block.
4. Sew the strips to the blocks, aligning the raw edges. Press the seams away from the block.
5. Measure the block across the middle to calculate the length of the strips needed for the other two sides and add two seam allowances ($\frac{1}{4}$", 0.75 cm).
6. Cut two folded strips the length determined in Step 5 for each block. Fold over and press the seam allowance ($\frac{1}{4}$", 0.75 cm) at each end.
7. Join the raw edges of these strips to the edges of the block, taking extra care when stitching across the folded-over seam allowances at each end.
8. Press. You should now have a framed block with a folded edge.
9. Pin or baste the block to the background fabric in the

appropriate position and stitch with thread that matches the frame (or use a contrasting color to create a decorative effect).

10. Fold the corners of the seam allowance edges by 45° so they don't show on the top. Use a blind stitch for hand appliqué. For machine stitching, use a straight stitch, zigzag, or decorative stitch.

11. If the quilt is to be machine quilted, it is not necessary to cut away the background fabric from behind the blocks. For hand quilting, cutting the back away will reduce the number of layers and make the quilting easier.

QUILTING THE QUILT

When the quilt top is complete, it's time to add the batting and backing and stitch the three layers together with quilting stitches. Decide whether to hand quilt, tie, or machine quilt the quilt. For basic instructions in hand quilting and tying, refer to pages 22-24.

Cut the batting and backing at least 1½" (4 cm) larger than the quilt top on all sides. The backing may be pieced, but for hand quilting keep the number of seams to a minimum. There are several types of batting available, ranging from 100% polyester to 100% cotton, poly/cotton mixes, and wool. For hand quilting, choose a batting without a scrim that is robust enough to allow the quilting lines to be up to 6" (15 cm) apart. For machine quilting, I recommend Warm and Natural batting - a low-loft cotton batting with a scrim that may be quilted with stitching lines as far apart as 10" (25 cm).

The quilting stitches hold the three layers together and are a vital part of the quilt. They may be used to enhance the appearance of the quilt or may be stitched "in the ditch" along the seam lines where they will be functional but not visible. First the quilt must be basted to hold the three layers together during quilting.

BASTING THE "QUILT SANDWICH"

Basting stitches hold the three layers of the quilt together until the quilting is completed, and are then removed. Baste with long running (basting) stitches, safety pins, or by using a basting gun with plastic tacks. I prefer basting stitches. The basting takes longer but the stitches don't rust like some safety pins, or get in the way while you are quilting. Basting is much more enjoyable if it is made into a social occasion with a reward of tea or dessert at the end! I am grateful to all the friends who helped me baste the children's quilts. We had fun and the job was done quickly and efficiently.

1. Press the quilt top and the quilt back (the seams on the quilt back may be pressed open).
2. Lay the quilt back flat, wrong side up, on a table (with a nonscratch surface or one you don't mind scratching), hard floor, or low-pile carpet. I use a table for small quilts and baste large quilts on the floor.
3. Tape the quilt back to the surface with masking tape or use T-pins on a carpet. Secure the opposing sides, working from the center out to the corners. Do the same for the

other two sides. Make sure the quilt back is perfectly flat. It should be taut but not stretched so that it is distorted.
4. Place the batting on top of the backing. Smooth it out so that there are no wrinkles.
5. Place the quilt top, right side up, over the batting. Make sure it is positioned centrally over the quilt back and that there is a margin of quilt back and batting exposed around each edge (at least 1½", 4 cm). Check that it is perfectly flat and square. Straight seams sometimes appear a little crooked and the quilt top may be gently manipulated to align them correctly.
6. If you are working on the floor, T-pin the quilt top in the same way as the quilt back. On a table, put safety pins in the corners and the center of each side through all three layers. Use a dessert or grapefruit spoon to help lift the end of the pin up from the surface so you can easily secure it.

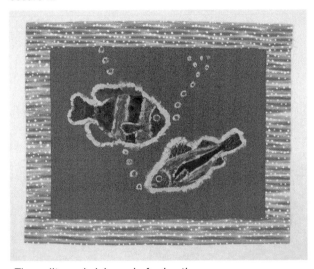

The quilt sandwich ready for basting.

7. Use quilting or regular thread, a large needle, and a spoon to lift the needle from the surface. Baste a grid of large running stitches all over the quilt. Start in the middle of one side of the quilt and baste all the way across. You may knot the thread or make a couple of backstitches at

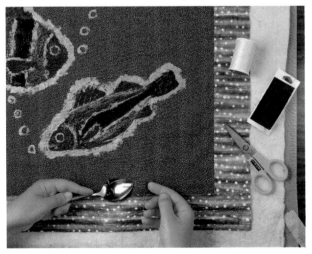

Use a spoon to help lift the end of the needle from the surface.

the beginning. Take four or five stitches before pulling the thread all the way through. This saves time, especially if your thread is long. For very large quilts, start in the center and baste to the edge. The second line of basting stitches should be about a hand's width away from the first. Continue basting the lines until you are near the edges of the quilt. Then baste at right angles, creating a grid of stitches.

8. Remove the tape or pins from the edges and baste all the way around the quilt ¼" to ½" (0.75-1.5 cm) from the edges.

9. To protect the batting and edges, roll the backing over to the front and baste it down. Now the quilt is ready to be quilted.

MACHINE QUILTING

For straight line quilting use a walking foot on your machine. The walking foot moves the three layers through the machine evenly and helps prevent tucks and bumps. For free-motion machine quilting, drop the feed dogs on the machine and set the stitch length and width dials to zero. Use a darning or free-motion embroidery foot. The way you move the fabric and the speed you run the motor will determine the stitch length and pattern. For help with machine quilting, refer to Maurine Noble's book *Machine Quilting Made Easy!* or take a class. It requires a little practice, but after two or three hours you will be proficient enough to tackle your quilt.

When the quilting is finished, remove all the basting stitches except those ¼" to ½" (0.75 to 1.5 cm) from the edge. These help to stabilize the edge while you add the binding. Remove them after the binding has been machine stitched and before it is hand stitched to the back.

FINISHING THE QUILT

Finishing touches improve the appearance of the quilt and can add special appeal. For example, the *Helping Hands Banner* on page 79 includes an appliquéd rabbit in addition to all the children's hands. Samson, the class bunny, was an important member of the group and the children wanted to include him on the quilt. On the *History of Bainbridge Island* quilt on page 42, the fabric used for the island was too close in value to the sea fabric so we stitched a white cord around the coastline to define the outline. A small detail like this can make a huge difference in the visual impact of a quilt.

You may want to add embellishments such as embroidery, charms, sequins, yarn, or anything you can attach with stitches (or glue if you want to risk having it fall off!). *Catch This* (page 59) has a plastic camera, shells, a crab's leg, and glass sewn onto it, and *Octopus's Garden* (page 57) has a fish-hook with a rubber worm. Be as creative as you like!

BINDING THE QUILT

Binding strips may be cut on the straight grain of the fabric unless the quilt has curved or irregular edges. I recommend a French (double) binding since it is strong and durable and finishes the quilt with a firm edge.

Attaching French binding to a quilt.

1. Calculate the number of binding strips needed by measuring the perimeter of the quilt and dividing by 40 (100 for metric) for fabric 42" (106 cm) wide.

2. Cut 2½" (7 cm) wide binding strips.

3. Cut the ends of the strips at 45° angles and join them together.

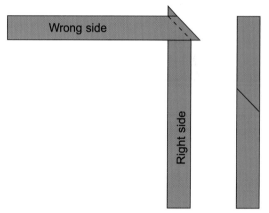

4. Press the seams open and press the binding in half lengthwise with the wrong sides together.

5. The quilt should be quilted, but still have basting stitches ¼" to ½" (0.75 to 1.5 cm) from the outer edge. Align the raw edge of the binding with the raw edge of the quilt top. Start stitching about 10" (25 cm) below a corner, leaving a tail of 6" to 8" (15 to 20 cm) of binding for joining at the end. Use a walking foot if you have one. If not, use a regular presser foot. Stop ¼" (0.75 cm) from the first corner, make three or four backstitches, and remove the quilt from the sewing machine.

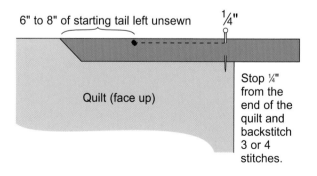

6. Rotate the quilt a quarter turn and fold the binding straight up, away from the corner, making a 45° angle fold. Bring the binding straight down in line with the next raw edge to be sewn. The top fold of the binding should be even with the edge just sewn.

Flip the binding straight up.

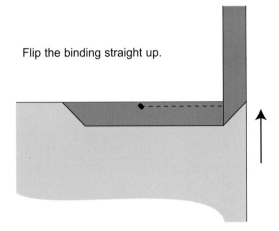

7. Start stitching with backstitches right to the edge of the top fold, then stitch until you reach the next corner. Stop and backstitch. Continue for all sides of the quilt.

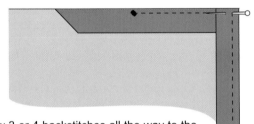

Sew 3 or 4 backstitches all the way to the edge, then proceed forward to the next corner.

8. Fold the binding at the corner as previously described and pin it by the top fold.

9. Trim the end of the binding to join it with a 45°angle seam to the 6" to 8" (15 to 20 cm) tail you left at the start. Open the binding ends and draw a pencil line at 45° where they join. Cut the tail ½" (1.5 cm) away from the line to accommodate the seam allowance. Stitch the binding ends together and finger press the seam open.

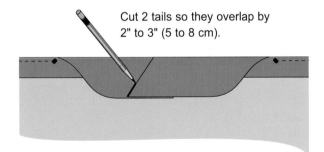

Cut 2 tails so they overlap by 2" to 3" (5 to 8 cm).

Open the 2 tails and place the end under the starting tail to match the diagonal cut of the starting tail.

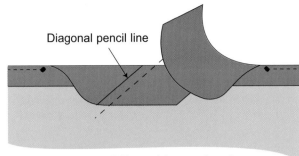

Diagonal pencil line

Cut the ending tail ½" (1.5 cm) longer than the diagonal pencil line.

10. Stitch the binding down, beginning with the backstitches at the corner and continuing until you meet the starting point.

11. Remove the basting stitches.

12. Use a rotary cutter or scissors to trim the excess batting and backing flush with the quilt top and binding raw edge. Your binding should be stuffed evenly with batting, so trim carefully.

13. Bring the folded edge of the binding to the back of the quilt so it covers the machine stitching line. Hand stitch it down with a blind stitch, pinning a small section at a time to hold it in place as you sew. Use thread that matches the binding rather than the quilt back.

14. Miter the corners by folding the unstitched binding from the next side over to form the 45° angle (it's rather like wrapping a parcel).

Another way to bind is to machine sew the binding onto the back of the quilt, then bring it to the front and top stitch with a decorative machine stitch.

The binding on Forest Fantasy *was top stitched for decorative effect.*

A third way is to fold the edge of the back of the quilt to the front and stitch it down. Make sure the backing is a coordinating fabric. Cut the batting flush with the edge of the quilt top. Cut the back at least 1" (2.5 cm) larger on each side than the quilt top. Fold over ½" (1 cm) on each edge and press. Bring this folded edge forward and pin it to the quilt top, then stitch it down using a machine with a walking foot or a hand blind stitch. Sew the two longest opposite sides first, then fold and sew the other two sides with a miter at the corners so no raw edges are exposed.

MAKING A LABEL

Labeling the quilt is an important finishing touch. Years from now, people will be curious about who made the quilt, and when and where. The label may be embroidered or written with fabric markers. Use a pale fabric so the words show clearly. If you are using markers, iron freezer paper to the back to stabilize the fabric while you are writing.

Include the following information on your label: quilt title, name of group (school, class, organization), names of all the participants, date, and location.

Labels for the back of the quilt.

A narrow colored frame may be added to the label to make it look more distinctive. Use a blind appliqué stitch in thread matching the frame to attach the label to the back of the quilt. I usually position the label in a lower corner of the quilt where it is easy to see by lifting the corner when the quilt is hanging.

MAKING A SLEEVE TO HANG THE QUILT

The easiest way to hang a quilt is to attach a sleeve to the back along the top edge. The sleeve is a fabric tube wide enough to accommodate a dowel. The dowel may be hung on hooks or suspended by fishing line from museum-style hangers on the wall. The hanging sleeve may be made from plain muslin or a fabric that matches the quilt back.

1. For a 4" (10 cm) wide sleeve, cut a fabric strip 8½" (22 cm) wide and 2" (5 cm) shorter than the quilt top.
2. Turn ½" (1.5 cm) to the wrong side of each short end and machine stitch.
3. Fold the sleeve in half lengthwise, with the right sides together, and machine stitch the raw edges. Turn right side out and press.
4. Pin the sleeve to the quilt back at the top, 1" (2.5 cm) below the binding.
5. Blind stitch the sleeve to the quilt, taking care that your

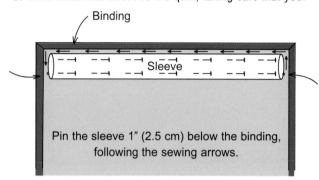

Pin the sleeve 1" (2.5 cm) below the binding, following the sewing arrows.

Stop sewing 1" (2.5 cm) from the lower edge of the sleeve.

stitches don't pass all the way through the quilt and show on the front. Start 1" (2.5 cm) from the lower edge of one end of the sleeve, stitch across the top, and down the other edge, stopping 1" (2.5 cm) from the bottom. Now the sleeve is sewn on three sides.
6. Reposition the fold in the sleeve and the pins. Move the sleeve up so that the top fold is just below the binding and pin it in place.
7. Blind stitch along the bottom edge. Remove the pins.

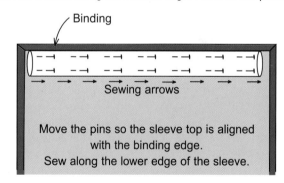

Move the pins so the sleeve top is aligned with the binding edge.
Sew along the lower edge of the sleeve.

This method eliminates any bulging on the front of the quilt around the dowel.
8. Hang the quilt and enjoy!

Chapter Four

Projects

Introduction

Each project lists a recommended minimum age, a detailed supply list, and instructions. Note that measurements in the supply lists are the *cutting sizes* for the parts of the quilt shown (block, sashing, border, etc.). The *finished sizes* will be ¼" (0.75 cm) smaller on each side due to the seam allowance. The standard seam allowance of ¼" (0.75 cm) should always be used. You may adjust the sizes to fit your particular project. Many of the general supplies (see page 10) are assumed and are not listed every time.

For those of you who teach children using the metric system, metric measurements are included with the directions for the quilts. Since rational imperial units do not translate into easy whole number metric units, metric equivalents, which will work, are used. My resource for these was the book *Metric Quiltmaking* by Margaret Rolfe with Beryl Hodges and Judy Turner, which you too may find useful. The templates in Appendix 6 do not include metric measurements, but for hand piecing projects you should be able to use them as is.

Refer to previous chapters to help you with your project. Chapter One will help you choose the appropriate project. Chapter Two provides instructions for marking fabric for sewing, hand sewing patchwork, appliqué and simple embroidery stitches, machine sewing, and quilting. Chapter Three includes general information and techniques used in quilt making to help you with the basics of making your quilt.

You may copy the projects in this book or modify them, choosing your own themes and combinations of techniques to fit the numbers, skill levels, and interests of your children.

Maggie training volunteers.

Any project will run more smoothly with the help of volunteers. For most of our group projects there were one or two volunteers present (in addition to the teacher) and myself. There was always a minimum of two adults working with the children. Extra help makes a huge difference, especially if there are children with special needs in the group, the children are sewing, or if they are using paint. Ask the volunteers to come a few minutes early so you have time to explain the project to them. Volunteer helpers for teaching hand sewing should be trained in advance to ensure that all the children learn the correct way. Trust me, untrained well-meaning volunteers can cause problems and take valuable time away from the children!

Here are some quick reminders before you dig into your project:

● Pre-washed 100% cotton fabric is recommended. Other fabrics and materials may be used for appliqué and embellishment.
● Use a consistent seam allowance of ¼" (0.75 cm).
● Allow additional time for choosing and purchasing supplies, training volunteers, a presentation introducing the children to quilts and quilting, assembling, quilting, and finishing the quilt.
● Ensure adequate supplies for the children and be prepared for the unexpected. Cut a few extra blocks as spares. For example, cut 23 blocks for 20 children, 15% extra, which should be enough.
● Be flexible. Sometimes projects take longer than expected or there are scheduling conflicts.
● Don't forget to add a label to the back of the quilt and include the names of all the participants.

The instructions given include estimates for the number of sessions required to complete the project, assuming 40-minute sessions unless otherwise specified. The preparation times given are approximate and assume that the fabric is already washed, supplies are on hand, and a rotary cutter is used.

If you are working with individuals or small groups you will be able to give more attention to each child, and it will be easier to demonstrate and involve the children in all the steps. Individual projects require a high level of commitment from the children because they take a relatively long time to complete. You should have at least one adult per six children to ensure that each child is given adequate individual attention.

Involve the children in the choice of materials, especially if the final product will remain in their possession. Children usually have definite ideas about which colors they like and a favorite hobby or theme (horses, dinosaurs, etc.), which they may like to incorporate. They will enjoy a shopping trip to the fabric store or the opportunity to rummage through your fabric stash and scrap bag. By all means make suggestions and offer alternatives if you feel strongly that the child's choice is unsuitable.

When scheduling projects, try to set some goals so the project progresses. A deadline or some incentive to finish the project is useful. Maybe the quilt will be given as a gift, entered into a show, or exhibited. Be prepared to be flexible. Children work at different rates and may miss sessions due to illness or time conflicts. Encourage the children to help each other.

With small groups, you can give each participant more attention. Here, a Camp Fire group displays their work in progress.

Supplies

Fabrics: The children's drawings and writing will stand out clearly on pale fabrics. You may use just one fabric, or include a variety. Unbleached muslin, pastel solids, and pale monochromatic prints work well. If you already have a theme fabric, choose coordinating colors. Good choices are pale green, pale blue, fawn, and unbleached muslin. Pure white is rather stark, but can be appropriate. Yellow should be used with care. A soft yellow can provide brightness, but a strong yellow will dominate and may detract.

Freezer paper: Use freezer paper to stabilize the fabric blocks or panels by ironing the waxed side to the wrong side of the fabric. Not only does this prevent the fabric from shifting and distorting while the children are drawing and writing, but the designs may be drawn on the paper and traced directly onto the fabric. Pencil drawings may be made, erased, and redrawn until they are just right. Then the fabric backed with freezer paper may be placed on a light table, an overhead projector, or taped to a window, for the picture to be traced onto the fabric side.

Attach the freezer paper to the fabric by ironing the two together before you cut the blocks or panels. To do this, first press the fabric, then place the shiny side of the freezer paper down on the wrong side of the fabric and iron gently (cotton setting). The wax melts and sticks to the fabric so the freezer paper becomes attached to the fabric. Turn it over to make sure the fabric is smooth and without wrinkles. If there are bumps, simply peel the freezer paper away when it is cool and try again. You may also press it from the fabric side. Cut the freezer paper-backed fabric to the desired size for the children to illustrate. If the freezer paper starts to come off while the children are working, it may easily be ironed back in place. The freezer paper is removed when the children are finished, and can be recycled for your next project.

Markers, crayons, etc.: For the illustrating, I recommend fabric markers (Marvy), crayons (Pentel Fabricfun pastel dye sticks), and acrylic paints (Scribbles). These are all easy to use, relatively clean, and the colors are bright. The markers are ideal for writing, outlining, touching up, and coloring small areas. The crayons work well for coloring large areas. However, the colors smudge easily before they are heat set, so the children's art should be handled with care. Heat set as soon as possible by covering the fabric with a piece of paper and using a very slow moving hot iron. Acrylic paints (Scribbles) are available in plastic bottles with fine nozzles. The paint may be gently squeezed from the bottle directly onto the fabric. These are good for outlining and embellishing but should be used sparingly to avoid blobs or a thick ridge of paint that may crack when the quilt is folded or washed. You can also purchase these in regular bottles, and apply them with a brush, but this is messier.

There are variety of markers, pens, chalk, and paints that work well on fabric.

If you are unable to obtain freezer paper to stabilize the fabric, use heat transfer crayons (Crayola). Make the drawings on nonglossy paper using the crayons, then transfer the image to the fabric by ironing. For the best results, synthetic fabric or a blend containing at least 50% synthetic fibers should be used. The colors are not as vibrant, but the problem of drawing on fabric that is not stabilized is avoided.

Drawing on freezer paper-backed fabric.

If you use other fabric paints, water-based or acrylic, read the instructions carefully. Many are designed as general "crafts" products, and you will need to add a textile medium to use them on fabric. Some products need to be heat set, or allowed to dry for several hours before the colors are fast.

Children should roll up their sleeves, and if possible, wear aprons when using paints or crayons. Most of these products will wash out of clothing before they dry or are heat set. However, I can't guarantee that clothing will not be stained!

Block Sizes and Shapes

Select a block size large enough for the children to draw a picture or write a few sentences. If you make the blocks too big, you will have an enormous quilt when you join 20 or 30 together! Squares between 5" (12 cm) and 10" (25 cm) work well. Cut the fabric to the required finished block size plus ¼" (0.75 cm) on each side for the seam allowance. For example, a block cut 7" x 5" (18 x 12.5 cm) becomes a 6½" x 4½" (16.5 x 11 cm) finished block. Use a rotary cutter (adults only) to quickly and accurately cut all fabrics. The blocks may be any shape and may be cut in a variety of sizes for a single quilt. Squares and rectangles are the easiest. You could make a large central panel with smaller blocks around the outside as was done on *Save the Rain Forest* (page 47) and the three historical Bainbridge Island quilts (pages 40-44).

Drawing on Freezer Paper-Backed Fabric

When you distribute the freezer paper-backed fabric to the children, ask those age eight or older to use a pencil and ruler to create a ½" (1 cm) margin all the way around the edge, on the paper side. For younger children, adults should create this ½" (1 cm) frame in advance. The children may write their name or a title in this margin on the freezer paper. Instruct them to keep all their drawings inside the box on the paper. If they draw in the margin all the way to the edge of the block, their design will be partially devoured when the blocks are sewn together. They may draw their picture outlines using pencil on the paper and erase as much as they want.

Check the drawings and encourage the children to fill the space. A tiny picture in one corner will not work! Once you and they are satisfied with the images, they can

Images on freezer paper and fabric. Note that the picture is reversed when it is traced onto the fabric.

darken the pencil lines for tracing (a fine-tipped black marker may be used for this). Next, tape the work fabric-side-up to a window or place it on an overhead projector or light table. Then have the children trace their drawing with pencil or fabric markers onto the fabric. This technique avoids the problem of accurately copying the image from a practice sheet directly onto the fabric without being able to correct mistakes. However, note that the image is reversed, so it does not work for writing! Before they start drawing, tell the children that the final image on the fabric will be the reverse of the image they draw on the freezer paper. Most of them are not concerned, but some are rather particular!

Taping the drawn design to the window makes it easy to trace on the fabric.

If there's writing on the blocks, a different method must be used, since tracing from the freezer paper onto the fabric reverses the image. Ask the children to write the words on a separate piece of paper. Place this with the freezer paper-backed fabric on top, on a light table or overhead projector (easier than a window since they are horizontal surfaces), then trace the letters. Alternatively, draw lines for writing guides on the freezer paper. Use the light table or overhead projector so the lines are visible, and write directly on the fabric without tracing the letters.

An overhead projector provides a good way to trace this map.

Making historical quilts is a wonderful way to bring together many different aspects of history and geography investigated by the children. Our children studied the local area, Bainbridge Island, but a project of this type could be extended to a wider region such as a county, state, or nation. The fourth graders at Wilkes School also used their mathematical knowledge to calculate the layout of the historical facts that surround the large central panel, and they used their fine motor skills to appliqué the Island and various landmarks.

Historical Bainbridge Island.

Bainbridge Island Past and Present.

History of Bainbridge Island.

Quilt 1
Historical Bainbridge Island
60" x 72" (150 x 180 cm)

Quilt 2
Bainbridge Island Past and Present
52" x 56" (155 x 140 cm)

Quilt 1, *Historical Bainbridge Island,* was predominantly based on events that occurred in the 19th century. We chose to use sepia and brown fabrics to give it an "old" look. Quilt 2, *Bainbridge Island Past and Present,* illustrated 1900 to the present day and we used multicolored fabrics. There is some historical overlap between the two. Both quilts featured a large map in the center and five topic paragraphs, each accompanied by four or five illustrations.

The children worked for three sessions. In Sessions I and II they made their illustrations and the map and in Session III they wrote the topic paragraphs.

First the children made a rough sketch of their block picture on paper that was the same size as the block. They could choose either a horizontal or vertical format for their illustration. After we checked the drawing, they drew it on freezer paper attached to the back of the fabric block, traced it with black marker onto the fabric, and colored with fabric markers and crayons to complete the block.

Small groups of three children worked on the maps. For Quilt 1, the Island outline was traced at a large window with good light. A map overlaid with the freezer paper-backed fabric panel was taped to the window so the children could easily see to trace the outline. For Quilt 2, the map was generated by projecting the image of a map from an overhead projector onto a piece of fabric backed with Steam-a-Seam 2 taped to the wall. The Island outline and roads were traced with a black fabric marker, then more details were added later. The completed Island was cut out and fused onto a sea background.

In the third session, the groups discussed and wrote their topic paragraphs. One child was nominated from each group to trace the paragraphs from lined paper onto the freezer paper-backed fabric blocks at an overhead projector.

Historical Bainbridge Island was pieced, and in *Bainbridge Island Past and Present* the blocks were framed and appliquéd. I recommend appliqué, which is much easier and less time-consuming than the complex piecing of the different sized blocks (see page 31 for instructions). Attempt the piecing only if you are experienced and enjoy pattern drafting.

Project participants:
48 children (24 on each quilt) ages 6 to 10, The Family Classroom, spring 1997
Minimum recommended age: 7
Difficulty level: Easy to moderate

Sessions: 2 or 3
Preparation: 1 to 2 hours per quilt (iron freezer paper onto fabric, cut blocks and central panel, mark margins on freezer paper)

Supplies
(see page 25 to estimate fabric quantities)
* Pale fabric for pictorial blocks, 7" x 5" (18 x 12.5 cm)
* Pale fabric for topic paragraphs, 6" square (15 cm)
* Fabric panel for map
  Quilt 1: 30" x 17½" (75 x 45 cm)
  Quilt 2: 31½" x 18" (79 x 46 cm)
  Both originally cut larger and trimmed to size after children's work was completed

* Solid color fabrics for framing blocks
* Fabric for background
* Fabric for binding and backing
* Steam-a-Seam 2 (if using fusible appliqué for map as in Quilt 2)
* Freezer paper to stabilize blocks and map panel
* Fabric markers
* Fabric crayons
* Batting

Quilt 3
History of
Bainbridge Island
73" x 51½" (183 x 130 cm)

Like the other two Bainbridge Island quilts, this one had a large map in the center. The children appliquéd the Island onto the background and also appliquéd several landmarks in the appropriate geographical positions. The historical facts were written with fabric markers on panels arranged in chronological order around the perimeter. Those panels placed along the top and bottom borders were vertical, and those at the sides were horizontal. With the help of their teacher, the children used paper, index cards, and their mathematical skills to calculate the configuration of the quilt.

The children worked on their quilt over a period of three weeks, mostly in small groups concentrating on different aspects. Parent volunteers helped three or four children at a time to appliqué the Island and the landmarks. The landmarks were drawn and colored using fabric markers and crayons. Another group calculated the configuration, while other children gathered the historical facts.

We allowed four sessions for hand sewing and another two sessions for drawing the landmarks, writing the historical facts, and working on the layout.

To make the appliqué Island, the children enlarged a map of Bainbridge Island and traced the outline onto the nonadhesive side of fusible interfacing. Then they used the appliqué technique described on page 19.

When the quilt top was nearly complete, it was apparent that some modification was necessary to enhance the visibility of the Island because the shoreline boundaries appeared to melt into the sea. A narrow white cord was sewn around the outline. This defined the Island clearly and greatly improved the visual impact of the quilt.

Project participants: 26 children ages 9 and 10, fourth grade, Wilkes School, spring 1994
Minimum recommended age: 8
Difficulty level: Challenging
Sessions: 5 or 6 - be flexible to allow time for hand sewing (appliqué)

Preparation: 2 to 3 hours (iron freezer paper onto fabric, cut blocks and landmarks fabrics, cut central sea panel, machine stitch interfacing to Island fabric and turn, fuse to sea background)

Supplies
(see page 25 to estimate fabric quantities)
* Fabric for large central panel for map, 51" x 30" (127 x 75 cm)
* Fabric for blocks for historical facts, 3½" x 5½" (9.5 x 13.5 cm)
* Unbleached muslin for landmarks on Island, 2½" square (6 cm)
* Fabric for borders
    3 around central panel, 2", 1¼", and 2½" wide (5, 3, and 6 cm)
    outer strawberry border, 4¼" wide (10.5 cm)

Distance between historical facts panels needs to be calculated according to layout
* Fabric for binding and backing
* White cord for outlining Island
* Fabric markers
* Fabric crayons
* Freezer paper to stabilize historical fact blocks and muslin for landmarks
* Lightweight fusible interfacing for appliqué
* Batting

ILLUSTRATED POETRY QUILTS

Children's poetry is delightful and brings smiles to those who read it. On a quilt, the poetry will survive and will be enjoyed for many years to come. Our children wrote poems about themselves. You may select any topic or let the children choose. Another idea is to use a story written by the children.

All About Me.

All About Me
60" x 48" (150 x 120 cm)

Project participants: 20 children ages 7 and 8, second grade, Wilkes School, spring 1994
Minimum recommended age: 7
Level of difficulty: Easy
Sessions with the children: 1 or 2
Preparation: 1 hour (iron freezer paper onto muslin and cut blocks)

Supplies (see page 25 to estimate fabric quantities)
* Unbleached muslin or pale fabric blocks for poems, 9½" square (24 cm)
* Fabric for sashing between blocks, 2½" wide (6 cm)
* Fabric for border, 4" wide (10 cm)
* Fabric for binding and backing
* Freezer paper for stabilizing poem blocks
* Fabric markers
* Batting

The children spent two sessions transferring their poems (composed earlier) onto the fabric blocks and illustrating using fabric markers. Some children finished in one class period, but many needed another session to add the finishing touches to their blocks. They wrote on the fabric in pencil first, then went over it with fabric markers.

You can draw lines on the freezer paper and place the block on a light table or overhead projector so the children can use the lines as a guide for their writing. Alternatively, the poem may be traced onto the freezer paper-backed fabric block from a separate sheet of paper (see page 39).

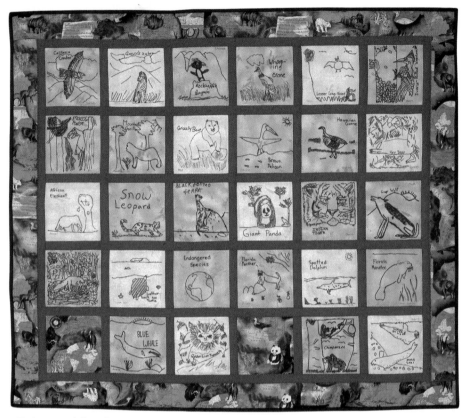

Endangered Species.

There are endless possibilities for creating pictorial quilts and it is easy to choose a theme appropriate to the children's interests or the class curriculum. The quilt may be made from blocks that are all the same size or be more complicated, with blocks of different sizes and large panels. Several examples are shown here. You may copy any of the configurations or adapt them to fit your particular project.

Endangered Species 45" x 51½" (115 x 129 cm)

Project participants: 27 children age 9 and 10, fourth grade, Wilkes School, spring 1994
Minimum recommended age: 7
Difficulty level: Easy to make the blocks, challenging to hand quilt

Sessions with the children: 1 or 2 for illustrating the blocks (add at least 5 sessions for hand quilting)
Preparation: 1 hour (iron freezer paper onto fabric, cut blocks)

Supplies
 (see page 25 to estimate fabric quantities)
* Pale fabric blocks for the animal drawings, 7" square (18 cm)
* Fabric for sashing between blocks, 1½" wide (4 cm)
* Fabric for border, 4" wide (10 cm)

* Fabric for binding and backing
* Freezer paper to stabilize blocks
* Black fabric marker pens
* Batting

After study and research, each child chose an endangered animal and drew its picture on a block using black fabric markers. First they drew the animals on freezer paper, then they traced them onto the fabric. Since 27 blocks is an awkward number to piece, three extra blocks were added - a title block and two made from printed theme fabric - for a total of 30. Parent volunteers worked with small groups of children at a quilt frame set up in the classroom. The children each hand quilted around their own block.

Save The Rainforest 64" x 41½" (160 x 104 cm)

Project participants: 25 children ages 8 and 9, third grade, Wilkes School, spring 1994
Minimum recommended age: 7
Level of difficulty: Easy to moderate
Sessions with the children: 2 or 3
Preparation: 1 to 2 hours (iron freezer paper onto fabric, cut blocks and large central panel)

Supplies
(see page 25 to estimate fabric quantities)
* Pale fabric for central panel, 19" x 35" (48 x 88 cm) Cut larger and trim to size to straighten edges and remove frays after the illustration is completed.
* Pale fabric for blocks, 5½" square (14 cm)
* Fabric for sashing between blocks, 1½" wide (4 cm)
* Fabric for borders
    around central panel, 1" wide (2.5 cm)
    inner yellow, 1½" wide (4 cm)
    outer rust, 5" wide (12 cm)
* Fabric for binding and backing
* Fabric markers
* Fabric crayons
* Freezer paper
* Batting

Save the Rain Forest.

The children had spent several weeks studying rain forests and built a three-dimensional tropical rain forest from recycled materials in their classroom, so this was an obvious theme for their quilt. The large central panel was a communal effort. The children drew the picture of the rain forest on freezer paper attached to the back of the fabric, then taped the panel to a window and traced the image on the cloth using pencils. They outlined it with color markers and colored it with fabric crayons. Each child chose a rain forest animal and illustrated a small block using fabric crayons and marker pens. The machine quilting stitches around the animals and the trees helped to accentuate the pictures.

The children spent one or two sessions drawing and coloring their animal blocks. Small groups were given additional time to work on the central panel. This took some time to complete, since it was complicated and every child contributed to the drawing or coloring.

Retreat Quilt 80" x 60" (200 x 150 cm)

Project participants: 50 children and adults ages 5 to 85, parishioners of St. Barnabas Episcopal Church, Bainbridge Island, September 1994 to September 1995
Minimum recommended age: 5, good project for a mixed age group

Level of difficulty: Easy to illustrate blocks, challenging to hand quilt
Sessions with the group: 1 or 2 to illustrate the 36 blocks; quilting completed over a 12-month period
Preparation: 2 hours (iron freezer paper onto fabric, cut blocks in variety of sizes)

Supplies
(see page 25 to estimate fabric quantities)
* Pale fabric for blocks
    4½" x 6½" (11.5 x 16.5 cm)
    4½" x 8½" (11.5 x 21.5 cm)
    6½" x 6½" (16.5 x 16.5 cm)
    6½" x 8½" (16.5 x 21.5 cm)
    8½" x 8½" (21.5 x 21.5 cm)
* Black fabric for framing blocks for appliqué, 1" wide strips make 1/4" frames

* Fabric for background - design your own to fit project finished size of cross 51½" x 31" x 10½" (128 x 76 x 6 cm)
* Fabric for border, 8½" wide (22 cm)
* Fabric for binding and backing
* Freezer paper to stabilize blocks
* Fabric markers
* Fabric crayons
* Batting

Retreat Quilt.

St. Barnabas Church held a family retreat at the seaside State Park at Fort Worden, Port Townsend, Washington, in September 1994. My family attended and I went prepared with freezer paper-backed fabric blocks, fabric markers, and crayons! I invited everyone at the retreat to participate and made the materials available for the whole weekend. During the first afternoon several children came and drew on quilt blocks and that evening they encouraged the adults to join in the project. The theme, "The Retreat," was broad and allowed plenty of room for interpretation by all!

Each block was framed with narrow black strips then appliquéd onto a large background pieced with a red cross on yellow and a blue border. See the instructions for appliquéing quilt blocks onto a background, page 31. The quilt was pieced and basted in time for the women's retreat in March 1995, where the hand quilting began (using a 14" embroidery hoop). Every Sunday thereafter, the parishioners (men, women, and children) continued the quilting during the social coffee hour after the morning service. Each week a parishioner took it home for hand quilting. The quilt was completed at the annual family retreat exactly one year after it was begun.

Self-Portrait Quilt 58½" x 58½"   (146 x 146 cm)

Self-Portrait.

One of the blocks in the Self-Portrait quilt.

The children drew the outlines of their portraits on a piece of paper in the first session. Parent volunteers traced the drawings, using pencil, onto the fabric. In the second session the children painted their pictures with the acrylic paints. A small number of colors was used and there were plenty of adults to help with brushes and supervision. Then black fabric markers were used to outline the drawings and several children wrote their names on their blocks.

Project participants: 24 children ages 5 and 6, kindergarten, Wilkes School, spring 1997
Minimum recommended age: 5 (children 7 or older can trace their own drawings)
Level of difficulty: Easy to moderate (painting needs high level of supervision - get extra help)
Sessions with the children: 2 or 3
Preparation: 1 hour if the children trace their own drawings, otherwise 2 to 3 hours (iron freezer paper onto fabric, cut blocks, trace children's drawings on fabric between first and second session)

Supplies
(see page 25 to estimate fabric quantities)
* Unbleached muslin blocks, 10" square (25 cm)
* Fabric for sashing between blocks, 2½" wide strips and 2½" squares at intersections (6 cm)
* Fabric for binding and backing
* Freezer paper to stabilize blocks
* Black fabric markers
* Acrylic fabric paint
* Batting

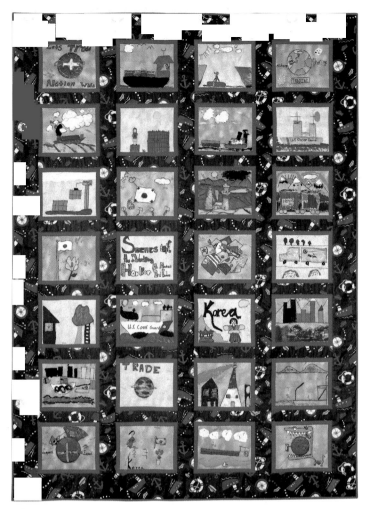

Scenes of a Working Harbor.

Scenes of a Working Harbor
83" x 61"
(208 x 152 cm)

One of the blocks in Scenes of a Working Harbor.

Project participants: 26 children ages 8 and 9, third grade, Wilkes School, spring 1994
Minimum recommended age: 8 (7 if markers and crayons are used instead of paint)
Level of difficulty: Challenging, extra help for supervision is necessary (Easy if markers and crayons are used instead of paint)

Sessions with the children: 3 to 5 (2 to 3 if using markers and crayons instead of paint)
Preparation: 1 hour (iron freezer paper onto fabric, cut blocks)

Supplies
(see page 25 to estimate fabric quantities)
* Pale fabric for blocks, 10" x 8" (24 x 20 cm)
* Fabric for framing blocks, 1¼" wide (3 cm)
* Fabric for sashing between blocks, vertical 3½" wide
   (9 cm), horizontal 2½" wide (6 cm)

* Fabric for border, 5" wide (12 cm)
* Fabric for binding and backing
* Freezer paper to stabilize blocks
* Fabric paints or fabric markers and crayons
* Fabric markers
* Batting

The children were studying ports and world trade, and in particular, trade with Korea. They toured a Hanjin container ship in the Port of Seattle. Each child used fabric paints to create a picture based on this theme. They touched up their paintings with fabric markers. The illustrations were drawn on the freezer paper and traced on the

fabric in pencil before the painting began.

The paints used, Delta Fabric Dyes, were water-based and colorfast when heat set. They came in small plastic bottles in box sets of eight colors and a textile medium. When I checked my local craft stores recently, I could not find this product. After reading of our experiences, I'm sure you will want to use fabric markers and crayons instead of paint! The paint had to be mixed with the textile medium to prevent it from bleeding into the fabric. We had 16 colors and we allowed four or five children at a time to illustrate their blocks. It was too confusing and not practical to have one paintbrush for each color, so instead we gave each child a brush. The problem was that they had to clean their brush before they changed color. If they put water in the paint, it bled on the cloth, so they had to dry their brushes as well as wash them. It was so stressful and time-consuming that we almost gave up! The colors looked bright, but it was tedious telling each child at least six times to wash and dry their brush between every color! Of course, we had a couple of disasters where the cloth acted like blotting paper when water was applied by accident, so we used some of our extra blank blocks.

A better way to do this would be to offer the children fewer colors and have one brush in each color. However, this type of project still needs rigorous supervision. Even if you work with small groups, expect a time-consuming event for the whole class to complete the project! It is messy and the paint may mark clothing, so the children should wear aprons or old clothes and roll up their sleeves. Our blocks were heat set with an iron and markers were used for touching up and outlining. I would not recommend this technique. The same vibrant colors may be reproduced using markers and crayons, which are much easier to use, are cleaner, and require less supervision.

Since 26 blocks is an awkward number to piece, two extra blocks were made and the 28 blocks were arranged in a 4 x 7 format (see page 30). Machine quilting stitches around the outlines of the pictures helped accentuate the illustrations.

Penguins on Parade 30½" x 40" (76 x 100 cm)

Penguins on Parade.

Project participants: The Ball family, all four of us, ages 9 to 42, 1994 to 1997!
Minimum recommended age: 7, good project for mixed age group

Level of difficulty: Easy
Sessions: Flexible, one block per person per session
Preparation: 1 hour (iron freezer paper onto pale fabric, cut into blocks)

Supplies
(see page 25 to estimate fabric quantities)
* Pale fabric for 9 illustrations, 7" square (18.5 cm)
* Theme fabric for 3 blocks, 7" square (18.5 cm)
* Fabric for framing strips, 24 @ 1" x 7" (2.5 x 18.5), 24 @ 1" x 8" (2.5 x 20.5 cm)

* Fabric for 31 sashing strips, 2½" x 8" (6.5 x 20.5 cm)
* Fabric for 15 intersecting squares, 2½" (6.5 cm)
* Fabric for binding and backing
* Freezer paper
* Fabric markers
* Batting

For *Penguins on Parade*, we ironed freezer paper onto the back of the fabric to stabilize the fabric while we drew. Remember that images drawn on freezer paper and traced through to the fabric will be reversed. Writing should be traced from a separate piece of paper. Refer to page 39 for the details of this technique and instructions.

My son Thomas was in the fourth grade at Wilkes Elementary School during the big quilt project of spring 1994. His class made the *Endangered Species* quilt (see page 46). Thomas chose to draw a rock-hopper penguin because penguins had fascinated him for some time. He suggested that if he made several penguin blocks, he could have his own penguin quilt to hang in his bedroom. I thought this was a grand idea, and the first block was a copy of the one he made for his class quilt. We recycled the freezer paper from the back of his class block, ironed it on a new block, and he traced it again. He had a T-shirt from the Boston Aquarium with nine different penguin pictures. We drew a couple of these, looked at pictures in books, and used our imagination.

I kept my eyes open for penguin fabrics and gathered a small collection. Thomas was most indignant that one of the fabrics showed penguins together with polar bears! He was irritated when his sister Hazel drew a block featuring both creatures, and he threatened to write "not" over the polar bear! The project became buried in my sewing room after we had drawn five blocks. It resurfaced again a couple of years later. We drew four more blocks, completing the nine illustrated blocks that appear on the quilt. The remaining three blocks were made from penguin theme fabrics.

You may adapt this project for a different theme. Take extra care when choosing the fabric to frame the blocks. A poor choice will result in the blocks merging into the background. I didn't originally plan to use hot pink on our quilt, but after laying the blocks next to several different colors, I found that the pink best highlighted and displayed the drawings.

My son Thomas with Penguins on Parade.

Supplies

Paints: We successfully used Deka water-based fabric paints, Versatex acrylic fabric paints, and Createx permanent fabric ink. These may be obtained from mail order art suppliers or ordered from art supply stores. I particularly like the Deka paints and highly recommend them. The colors are vibrant and include metallics that look wonderful. The paint is the right consistency for applying with brushes, sponges, or rollers. Neither the Deka nor the Versatex paints require the addition of a textile medium. If you buy "craft" paints, read the instructions carefully to make sure they are suitable for fabric. You may need to buy a textile medium to prevent the paint from bleeding on the fabric. Heat set most paints by ironing the fabric from the back side after allowing plenty of time for the paint to dry (at least three hours, preferably 24). Whatever products you use, *read the instructions carefully* and follow them!

Painting supplies. Spoon small quantities of paint onto paper plates for the children to use.

Children enjoy working with paint but should be warned that fabric paint is permanent and will mark their clothes unless it is washed out immediately! Most products will wash out if they have not yet been heat set (rinse as soon as possible in cold water, then wash as usual), but I can't guarantee that there will be no stains. Have the children wear aprons or old clothes with rolled up sleeves. Distribute the paint in small quantities on paper plates. This reduces waste from spills and two or three different colors may be placed on each plate. Brushes, sponges, and rollers should be clean and dry at the start of the project and washed thoroughly after use.

Fabric: Select pale-colored fabrics and brightly-colored paints so the prints stand out and the children's creative work is clearly visible.

Printing molds: For printing objects, choose items with distinctive contours to make interesting prints. We used a real octopus, real fish, and rubber marine animals (Nasco Life/Forms). Leaves, ferns, hands, and feet work well too.

Resist stencils: Freezer paper is needed to make the resist stencils.

Block printing tools: For block printing, specialty block cutting tools are necessary, as well as linoleum or Safety-Kut for the blocks. Safety-Kut is easy to cut. Linoleum is tougher but may be softened by heating (iron it!). The cutting tools (Speedball) are sharp, so be sure to teach the children how to use them properly. Safety must be emphasized when teaching and the children should be at least ten years old.

You may like to combine printing on your quilt with another project. For example, allow the children to print on T-shirts they bring in, or print on small pieces of fabric the children can take home and keep.

FISH PRINTS

Making fish prints (gyotaku) is great fun and a special event for the children. If possible, extend your session to an hour or 90 minutes so you can complete all the printing in one session.

Fresh fish should be used as quickly as possible and will not keep! The children will soon get used to the smell and they will love every minute of it! If you plan to do another project at a later date, it is well worth investing in rubber fish (Nasco Life/Forms). These don't smell, are cleaner to use, and can be used again and again. You may print the fish on the background fabric or on separate pieces of fabric and appliqué the fish prints onto the background.

If planning more than one fish print project, invest in rubber fish.

Preparing the Whole-Cloth Background

For the whole-cloth background, choose pale fabric so the fish prints stand out. If dark fabric is used the colors of the paints will appear darker and not so vibrant. I like watery looking blues that have a little variation in color, but solid colors work too. You may use a plain background or create a seabed of rocks and weeds with fusible appliqué or machine appliqué.

For large quilts such as Quilts 1, 2, and 4 (pages 57, 58, and 60) make a full-size sketch of the seabed on butcher paper. Trace the weeds, rocks, and substrate from the sketch and cut them out from a variety of fabrics backed with fusible webbing (Steam-a-Seam 2 recommended). Where two pieces overlap, allow extra fabric along the edge of the piece that will be underneath. Fuse the pieces to the whole-cloth background by heat pressing with an iron or machine appliquéing. If you want to involve the children in this stage, schedule an additional session.

The dotted lines indicate overlap under the top layer.

Turn the sketch over and trace it through to create a reverse image. Use this as the background paper for arranging the placement of the fish at the time of printing. There is no need to do this if you decide to print the fish on separate pieces of fabric and appliqué them onto the background such as on Quilt 4 (page 60).

Sketch the marine background.

Trace the marine background onto the back of the paper to create a reverse image.

Painting and Printing the Fish

Place octopus and large fish on wooden boards or stiff cardboard and secure the legs and fins with small pieces of modeling clay. Use dry, soft brushes in good condition

The background fabric with the seabed on it.

to apply the paint. Stiff abused paintbrushes are hard to use and will result in a streaky print. Instruct the children to paint evenly all over the animals without any thick blobs or ridges of extra paint. The painted animals should be carefully lifted so as not to smudge or get fingerprints on the paint, and placed in position on the paper with the reverse sketch. The reverse sketch must be used so that when the background cloth is laid over the top with the right side down, the fish are in the correct place in relation to the weeds and substrate. Remember that for all creatures facing the left on the reversed paper sketch, their prints will face to the right, and vice versa.

Painting the octopus.

Take extra care when placing the background cloth over the painted fish, especially when the piece is large. An adult at each end or a responsible child at each corner will work. Lower the cloth from above, with the right side down, and make sure it is positioned exactly over the paper with the painted fish. Gently bring it down to touch the fish on the paper, then release the ends or corners.

Placing the fabric on top of the painted fish.

Gently press the fabric over the animals to make the print. Use the back side of a spoon or the palms and ball of the hand with slight, even pressure, rather than poking with fingertips. Fingertips may be used gently around the edges of the animals and on the fins to help with the definition. I was pleasantly surprised that even some of the leg suckers on the octopus showed up on our print.

The children gently press the fabric over the animals using hands and spoon backs.

Now for the best part! Watch the children's faces light up as you gradually lift the fabric up to expose the print. They are thrilled to see the images of the creatures they painted and the marine scene in its entirety. ("There's my starfish!" "Look at my purple fish!" "Isn't this cool!") Give yourselves a round of applause! Lay the cloth flat or pin it to the wall until the paint dries. Allow at least three hours (24 is better) before heat setting the paint by pressing the whole-cloth with a hot iron from the back side (follow the instructions for the paint used). If you used real fish, you will probably want to wash the cloth to eliminate fishy odors!

Alternatively, print only three or four critters at a time (as in Quilt 3) and organize the layout as you go along, without using the paper sketch described above. Start from one end of the quilt and carefully use a hair dryer to dry the paint quickly before the next printing. While you are doing this, the animals can be wiped with paper towels to remove residual paint and repainted by the next group of children. Lay the animals on a fresh

clean piece of paper for each printing. It's fun to watch the marine scene gradually develop and there will be excitement each time new critters are added.

Another method is to print the fish on separate pieces of fabric, preferably white or unbleached muslin (as in Quilt 4). The advantages of this are that the children can work more independently and if any of the prints are unsatisfactory, it is easy to make more. You don't have to decide where all the fish will be placed until after the prints are made and you can play around with various positions, adding more fish if necessary. Appliqué the fish to the background using fusible webbing or fusible interfacing with machine or hand stitching around the edges (see page 19 for instructions).

Finishing Touches

After the paint on the marine scene has dried, make sure you are satisfied with the visual impact and overall design. It's easy to add a couple more prints to improve and complete the picture. More appliqué pieces can also be added and positioned over the prints, so it appears, for example, that a fish is swimming behind seaweed.

Press and trim the edges of the whole-cloth to remove any frays and make the corners square. If you would like the fish to stand out from the surface, place an extra layer of batting behind them. When the quilt is assembled and quilted, you can add embellishments such as pieces of shell, crab claw, ceramic fish or charms, and a fishing line with hook and bait. Use your imagination and have fun!

After the lift-off!

Quilt 1
Octopus's Garden 49" x 88" (123 x 220 cm)

Octopus's Garden.

Quilt 2
Under The Sea 46" x 79" (114 x 198 cm)

Under the Sea.

Project participants: 26 children ages 9 and 10, fourth grade, Blakely School, spring 1997
Minimum recommended age: 7
Difficulty level: Easy to moderate. Extra volunteers recommended to help supervise painting.
Sessions: 1 extended session (it took us 1¼ hours to print both quilt tops) and a little extra time for a small group to complete tracing the writing on the fabric.

Preparation: 3 hours (draw sketch, trace reverse image, cut and fuse substrate and weeds on whole-cloth background, iron freezer paper onto border fabric for writing, cut) Only ½ hour of preparation is needed for a plain whole-cloth with no fused appliqué.

Supplies
(see page 25 to estimate fabric quantities)
* Large pale background cloth, 42" x 72" (105 x 180 cm)
* Pale fabric for writing in the border, 3½" wide (9 cm)
* Fabric for border
     Quilt 1: outer border, 5½" wide (14 cm)
     Quilt 2: strip between whole-cloth and writing, 1¼" wide (3 cm)
* Fabric for binding and backing
* Variety of substrate fabrics to create sea bottom and weeds

* Sheet of paper as large as background cloth for rough sketch of layout and placement of fish
* Steam-a-Seam 2 for fusing substrate
* Fabric paint
* Paintbrushes
* Fabric markers
* Fish (cabezon and rockfish), 24" octopus, rubber fish, crab, starfish
* Freezer paper to stabilize border strips for writing
* Batting

Proudly displaying their handiwork.

During the extended session, half the children painted fish while the others worked on their written words for the borders, then the groups switched after the first print was made. Each child in the class wrote four words from the Beatles' song "Octopus's Garden" on paper the same width as the quilt border. All the words were taped together in strips the same length as the sides and top of the marine scene. Then two children used a variety of colored fabric markers to trace them on the freezer paper-backed fabric border strips.

These marine scenes have great potential for intricate quilting patterns. An all-over meander stitch for the water works well (Quilt 2), as do waves (Quilt 1). Metallic threads enhance the appearance of the fish and make them sparkle. On *Octopus's Garden* we added a quilted fish hook with a rubber worm dangling in front of the large fish, technically not correct for marine fishing, but it brought chuckles!

Quilt 3
Catch This
56" x 50"
(140 x 125 cm)

The children worked in small groups of four or five to paint the animals and print. The scene was printed in several stages and a hair dryer was used to help dry the paint each time. In the second session the children wrote quotations and some of their own poems, using fabric markers on strips of freezer paper-backed fabric for the border.

The machine quilting was ornate. Metallic threads outlined the fish, shrimp, crabs, starfish, stars in the sky, and some of the rocks. The water was stipple quilted in blue thread. A little plastic camera, shells, a crab claw, and beach-combed glass were among the embellishments added, giving this delightful quilt additional character.

Catch This.

Project participants: 22 children ages 7 and 8, second grade, Wilkes School, spring 1994
Minimum recommended age: 7
Difficulty Level: Easy to moderate

Sessions with the children: 2 (1 to 1½ hours for printing and 45 minutes for writing)
Preparation: 3 hours (prepare whole-cloth background with machine appliqué, iron freezer paper onto pale border fabric for writing, cut)

Supplies
(see page 25 to estimate fabric quantities)
* Pale background cloth, 38" x 43" (95 x 108 cm)
* Variety of fabrics for sea bottom and weeds (machine appliquéd)
* Pale fabric for writing in border, 2¼" wide (5.5 cm)
* Fabric for border, parallelograms of varying lengths, 5½" wide (14 cm)
* Fabric for binding and backing
* Versatex acrylic paints
* Paintbrushes

* Hair dryer
* Fish (3 herring and a perch), starfish, shrimp, rubber crab
* Fabric markers
* Batting
* Embellishments (pieces of shell, crab claw, glass, driftwood, plastic camera, cord for fishing line)
* Fabric markers
* Batting

Quilt 4
Fantasy Coral Reef 44" x 79" (112 x 198 cm)

Fantasy Coral Reef.

Project participants: 24 children ages 13 and 14, eighth grade, Hyla Middle School, spring 1999
Minimum recommended age: 7 for printing only, 9 for cutting out substrate
Difficulty level: Easy to moderate.
Sessions with the children: 2 (1 for choosing and cutting the substrate, 1 for printing) Or 1 session if the children only do the printing.
Preparation: 1 hour (draw full-scale sketch of substrate, fuse substrate between first and second session) 3 hours if children are just printing and you need to cut and fuse substrate in advance.

Supplies
(see page 25 to estimate fabric quantities)
* Large pale background cloth, 42" x 72" (105 x 180 cm)
* Variety of substrate fabrics to create sea bottom and weed
* Plain white cotton, or unbleached muslin pieces of fabric for printing fish
* Fabric for border
    inner frame 1¼" wide (3 cm)
    outer border on 3 sides, 2" wide (5 cm)
* Fabric for binding and backing
* Sheet of paper as large as background cloth for sketch of substrate
* Steam-a-Seam 2 for fusing substrate (and fish if desired)
* Lightweight fusible interfacing for fusing fish
* Fabric paint
* Paintbrushes
* Rubber fish and turtle, starfish
* Batting

One group of 12 children selected the fabrics and cut the substrate from a variety of fabrics. They traced each part of the substrate from the full-scale sketch, then cut out the fusible-backed fabric. The substrate was fused before the second session, then the other group of 12 printed the fish onto pieces of plain white fabric.

The fish were appliquéd to the background with lightweight fusible interfacing (see page 19), then machine stitched around the edges during quilting. High-loft polyester batting was used so the fish would stand out from the surface, adding more depth to the quilt. However, this type of batting wasn't heavy enough for the fused substrate area and the quilt buckled along the bottom and didn't hang straight. Additional quilting in the substrate area helped, but the best solution to the problem was to sew a sleeve to the back at the bottom and insert a wooden dowel to add some weight and pull the quilt down. My advice is to use a denser batting with more body, like Warm and Natural, then cut out extra pieces of batting to put under the fish so they stand out from the surface.

Fishes and Best Wishes For M.J.
25" x 38"   (62 x 95 cm)

Fishes and Best Wishes for M.J.

Project participants: Hazel Ball, age 14, and Sushi Speidel, age 11, spring 1997
Minimum recommended age: 7
Level of difficulty: Easy to moderate

Sessions: 1
Preparation: 1 to 2 hours (cut background fabric, cut and fuse seabed)

Supplies
(see page 25 to estimate fabric quantities)
* Pale fabric for background, 23" x 34" (58 x 85 cm)
* Variety of fabrics for weed and sea bottom
* Fabric to frame 3 sides, 1" wide (2.5 cm)
* Fabric to border 3 sides, 3¼" wide (9 cm)

* Fabric for binding and backing
* Fabric paints
* Paintbrushes
* Rubber fish, starfish, crab
* Steam-a-Seam 2 for fusing substrate
* Batting

My daughter Hazel and friend Sushi enjoyed making the fish prints on this little quilt, which I gave to M.J. Linford as a thank you for working with me at Blakely School for five months. I created the seabed using fusible appliqué and drew a sketch to position the fish (see page 54). I quilted a meandering stitch in the water with variegated rayon thread and used silver metallic thread to highlight the fish.

Eric The Fish
20" x 20"   (50 x 50 cm)

Eric the Fish.

Project participants: Hazel Ball, age 14, spring 1997
Minimum recommended age: 7
Level of difficulty: Moderate

Sessions: 1 (1 to 1½ hours)
Preparation: 15 minutes (cut background fabric)

Supplies
(see page 25 to estimate fabric quantities)
* Pale fabric for background, 15" square (36 cm), trimmed
  to 14½" square (35 cm) after painting
* Fabric for frame, 1" wide (2.5 cm)
* Fabric for border strips, 3" wide (8 cm)

* Fabric for binding and backing
* Rubber fish (Eric)
* Fabric paints
* Paintbrushes
* Batting

First, Hazel printed "Eric." Instead of using fusible appliqué for the sea bottom, she painted the weed, rocks, and background. I had fun machine quilting different patterns on the rocks, and used silver metallic thread for the fish. The meander stitch in the water was done with variegated rayon thread.

Resist stencils are created using freezer paper cut into the desired shape and then ironed, shiny wax side down, onto blocks or larger pieces of fabric. Next, the fabric is sponge painted with fabric paint. The freezer paper resists the paint, preventing it from reaching the fabric. When the paint dries, the freezer paper shapes are peeled off, leaving a silhouette of the shape where there is no paint.

The results are pleasing and projects can be designed for a wide age range of children, increasing in complexity for older children. Preschool children enjoy sponge painting, and the fabric with freezer paper shapes may be prepared for them in advance. Older children can draw and cut out their own shapes from the freezer paper. Simple animal silhouettes made from drawing around cookie cutters or wooden craft shapes work well. More elaborate stencils, like snowflakes, can be created by folding and cutting the freezer paper. The freezer paper stencils may be recycled for other projects.

Printing

Choose pale-colored fabric, muslin, or white fabric. When the freezer paper resist stencils are ready, position and iron them, shiny side down, on the right side of the fabric. To apply the fabric paint, use small sponges (about 2", 5 cm, in diameter) that can be made by cutting up dish-washing sponges. The sponges are hard when dry and won't absorb the paint, so soften them first by moistening and squeezing out as much water as possible.

Dabbing a paint-filled sponge on the fabric.

Dab the sponges with paper towels to remove excess water. Place small quantities of paint on paper plates, two or three colors to a plate, with a sponge for each color. Supervise the children as they sponge paint all the exposed cloth, making sure they cover the whole piece right up to the paper, so the edge of the stencil will be clearly defined. The sponges should be used lightly, dabbing rather than scrubbing, with sufficient paint to cover the fabric. If the paint is applied too thickly, it saturates the fabric and goes through to the surface below. Remove as much water from the sponges as possible to prevent the paint from bleeding under the freezer paper

Children cutting snowflakes out of freezer paper.

Maggie and M.J. peeling off snowflakes.

The painted block with the resist shapes in place.

stencil, causing an indistinct edge around the resist print.

Beware! If you are painting a large whole-cloth, make sure the surface beneath is smooth. We tried one on three tables pushed together. When the paint dried, lines were visible where the tables joined, so we had to cut up the fabric into smaller pieces and discard some parts.

The painted fabric should be left to dry for at least two hours (preferably longer) before the freezer paper stencils are peeled away. The children will be excited to see their resist stencil prints.

After the resist shapes have been peeled off.

Three Snowflake Quilts

Project participants: 3 second grade classes (24 children in 2 classes, 25 in the other class) ages 7 and 8, Blakely School, spring 1997
Minimum recommended age: 7
Level of difficulty: Easy to moderate
Sessions with the children: 2, optional 3rd session for a follow-up project
Preparation: 1 to 2 hours (cut freezer paper squares, cut fabric for printing)

Supplies
(see page 25 to estimate fabric quantities)
These are general supplies for the three quilts shown. Specific block, sashing, and border sizes are given with each quilt.
* Pale fabric for making snowflake prints, large panels or individual blocks
* Dark contrasting fabrics for sashing and borders
* Fabric for binding and backing
* Freezer paper
* Iron
* Fabric paints: variety of blues, metallic and dark green, purple, silver
* Small sponges, about 2" in diameter (5 cm)
* Batting

In Session I, the children cut out their freezer paper snowflakes. Session II was spent painting. The snowflakes were arranged on the fabric by the children and an adult ironed them down during class time. We made prints on several different pale snowflake-patterned fabrics, all with pleasing results. In a third session, we recycled the freezer paper snowflakes, allowing the children to print their own little snowflake blocks to take home. Some children had their blocks fused onto a T-shirt and for the others, we fused them onto a piece of colored felt (using Steam-a-Seam 2). Teaching the children to make the freezer paper snowflakes was the most challenging part of the project.

Making the Snowflakes

Supplies
* Freezer paper squares 4", 5", 6" (10, 12, 15 cm) to make small, medium, and large snowflakes (enough for every child to have at least one of each size)
* Cardboard equilateral triangles, (3½"" (9 cm) from base to point)
* Pencils
* Scissors

Start with the largest square of freezer paper and progress to making smaller snowflakes once the children have mastered the technique. To make six-pointed snowflakes, the paper must be folded into sixths. This is difficult for seven year olds (the minimum recommended age), but with a little perseverance they can all be successful. Demonstrate two or three times to the whole group and be prepared to spend more time with those having problems. If possible, get extra volunteers to help.

Fold the freezer-paper square in half, with the shiny side inside. Fold it in half again, and then unfold this last fold. The fold mark is the center. Mark the center point with a pencil.

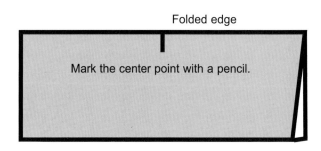

Folded edge

Mark the center point with a pencil.

Place the rectangle on the table with the folded edge closest to you. Place one point of the cardboard triangle by the center pencil mark, lining up the edge of the triangle with the folded edge of the paper. Draw a line along the edge of the triangle on the paper.

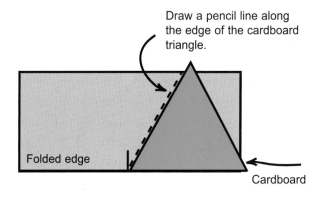

Draw a pencil line along the edge of the cardboard triangle.

Folded edge

Cardboard

Place one triangle point on the center mark and align the edge with the paper fold.

Move the triangle to the other side of the center crease mark and repeat. Now you have a paper rectangle with a fold at the bottom and two pencil lines from the center at 60° angles. The pencil lines are your folding lines.

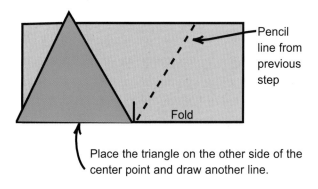

Pencil line from previous step

Fold

Place the triangle on the other side of the center point and draw another line.

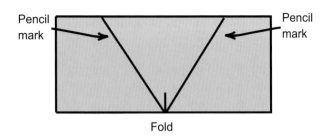

Pencil mark → ← Pencil mark

Fold

Fold along one pencil line, folding the flap toward you.

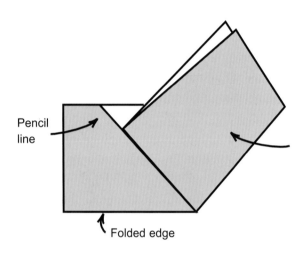

Pencil line

Folded edge

Holding the paper in the same position, fold along the other pencil line, folding the flap away from you. Now you have a wedge-shaped piece of folded paper and you are ready to start cutting.

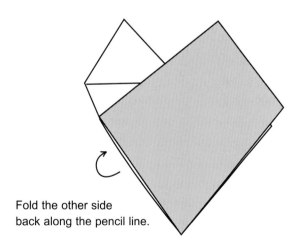

Fold the other side back along the pencil line.

Hold the wedge at the folded point. Start by cutting away the irregular pieces at the top in either a V-shaped valley or a pointed mountain.

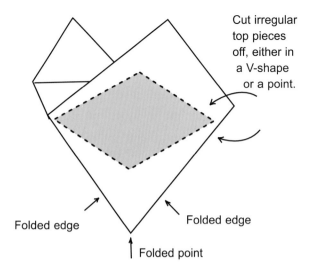

Cut irregular top pieces off, either in a V-shape or a point.

Folded edge   Folded edge

Folded point

Cut away pieces from the folded edges. For example, cut small wedges at any angle, half hearts, semicircles, half diamonds. Take care not to cut away the entire folded edge or your snowflake will disintegrate! Do not cut away the point of the wedge.

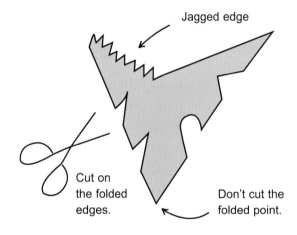

Jagged edge

Cut on the folded edges.

Don't cut the folded point.

Decorative edge scissors can be used to trim the top edges.

Further small cuts may be made in the top mountain or valley. Decorative edge scissors will give the snowflakes an interesting edge.

When the cutting is complete, open up the paper and examine the finished snowflake. This is fun. Watch the delight on the children's faces!

The finished paper snowflake.

Winter Wonderland
55½" x 55½"   (139 x 139 cm)

Winter Wonderland.

Supplies
(see page 25 to estimate fabric quantities)
See general supplies list on page 65.
* Pale snowflake-patterned fabric blocks, 9" square (24 cm)
* Fabric for sashing frames around each block, 1½" wide (4 cm)
* Fabric for outer border, 3½" wide (9 cm)
* Silver thread to zigzag stitch around outline of snowflakes for extra sparkle

The children printed two or three snowflakes on individual fabric blocks. They arranged the freezer paper snowflakes without any overlaps. Snowflakes placed across the edge of the block made partial prints.

Frosty Window 56" x 50"   (140 x 125 cm)

Frosty Window.

Supplies
(see page 25 to estimate fabric quantities)
See general supplies list on page 65.
* 4 pale snowflake-patterned fabric panels, 22½" x 25½"
  (56 x 64 cm). Cut them slightly larger, then trim after printing
  to remove frays from edges and to square corners.
* Fabric for frames around panels, 1¼" wide (3 cm)
* Fabric for sashing between panels, 2" wide (5 cm)
* Fabric for outer border, 2¼" wide (5.5 cm)
* Fabric for center circle, 4" diameter (10 cm)

The children worked in four groups to arrange and print their snowflakes on four large fabric panels. The panels were covered with meander quilting stitches in shiny translucent thread. When the quilting was completed, the middle of the quilt was distorted. This was successfully disguised by appliquéing the purple circle over the center. We agreed that this enhanced the look of the quilt. Sometimes modifications to an original design are necessary, and a quilt evolves in unexpected ways!

Winter Star.

Winter Star

45" x 45"
(114 x 114 cm)

The children printed their snowflakes on one large (36" x 42", 90 cm x 106 cm) piece of fabric. After the paint dried, we noticed dark lines in a large T on the middle of the cloth, corresponding to the edges of the three tables we had pushed together for the project. The whole-cloth idea was scrapped, and we cut up the printed fabric, then pieced it into a large Ohio Star with border side panels. If you make the quilt using the metric measurements provided, the finished size will be 122 x 122 cm.

To make the Ohio Star, cut the pieces before printing and follow the directions below.

Supplies
See general supplies list on page 65.
* Pale fabric for printing, 1 yard/meter
* Dark contrasting fabric, 1 yard/meter (includes enough for binding)

Instead of snowflakes, you could print leaves or ferns for this project.

Cut the pale fabric, then print:
* 4 @ 9" (24 cm) square for corners of Ohio Star;
* 2 @ 9¾" (26 cm) square. Print before making diagonal cuts for the 8 triangles in Ohio Star;
* 4 @ 9" x 29" (24 x 77 cm) for border panels.
Cut the dark contrasting fabric:
* 5 @ 9" (24 cm) square - 1 for center of Ohio Star, 4 for border corners;
* 2 @ 9¾" (26 cm) square, cut diagonally both ways to make 8 triangles for Ohio Star;
* 2 @ 2" x 26" (5.5 x 69 cm) for inner frame around Ohio Star;
* 2 @ 2" x 29" (5.5 x 77 cm) for inner frame around Ohio Star.

To construct the star, follow the Ohio Star piecing instructions in Appendix 4. Add the inner border strips, first the two shorter ones on opposite sides, then the two longer ones on the other two sides. Join the side panels to the framed star. Sew the corner squares to the top and bottom panels, then join these strips to the star.

Exploring Childhood Preschool Quilt
37" x 37"   (92 x 92 cm)

Exploring Childhood Preschool Quilt.

Project participants: 12 preschool children ages 3 to 5, and 4 high schoolers ages 14 to 16, Bainbridge High School Exploring Childhood Preschool, spring 1997
Minimum recommended age: 3 - a high level of supervision is necessary for such young children, 1:1 or 1:2

Level of difficulty: Easy
Sessions with the children: 1 to paint, additional session if children tie the quilt
Preparation: 2 hours (cut blocks, draw and cut out freezer paper resist stencils, iron stencils onto blocks)

Supplies
(see page 25 to estimate fabric quantities)
* Pale fabric blocks, 7" (18 cm)
* Fabric for sashing, 1¾" wide (4.5 cm)
* Fabric for border, 3" wide (8 cm)
* Fabric for binding and backing
* Freezer paper

* Cookie cutters or wooden craft animals
* Fabric paint
* Paper plates
* Small sponges
* Embroidery floss for tying
* Batting

In the Exploring Childhood class, high school students were given the opportunity to organize projects for the preschool children. My daughter Hazel, 14, coordinated this project. She drew around cookie cutters and wooden craft shapes, then cut the freezer paper animal shapes and ironed them on the fabric blocks. The preschool children sponge-painted the blocks. Each child was allowed to select two or three fabric paints for their block and worked under the supervision of a high school student. The children also tied the quilt with embroidery floss.

BLOCK PRINTING

For this technique, I recommend that you have experience in making blocks and using the specialized tools. The cutting knives are sharp and safety must be emphasized when teaching the children. In the instructions, I assume that if you choose this project, you are familiar with the tools and the safe ways to cut the linoleum or Safety-Kut blocks. Most of the information provided pertains to the printing on fabric. If you would like to try this technique for the first time, ask for help from an art teacher or someone else with experience, and practice on your own before working with the children. The children should be at least ten years old.

Supplies and Recommendations

Printing tools.

I recommend Safety-Kut (available from art suppliers or mail order) for making the blocks. It has the consistency of a rubber eraser and is easy to cut. If you can't find Safety-Kut, use linoleum, which is harder to cut but may be softened slightly by heating it with an iron.

We used ink (Createx permanent black fabric ink) and fabric paint (Deka) to print. Both worked well and were problem-free. The ink is more likely to permanently stain clothing and is also more expensive than the paint, so my first choice is the Deka fabric paint. Both should be heat set by ironing the fabric on the wrong side (follow the manufacturer's instructions). The children should wear aprons or old clothes with rolled up sleeves. Soiled clothing should be rinsed as soon as possible in cold water before washing as usual. I can't guarantee that there will be no stains! Print on pale-colored fabric so that the designs show clearly.

Use a variety of cutting tools (Speedball) ranging from steep V's for fine work to shallow U's for scooping out large areas. Demonstrate safe use of these at the start of each session, then remind the children constantly while

they are working. They tend to turn their block and forget to place it next to the bench hook, cut towards themselves, or place their free hand in the line of cutting. A first-aid kit should be available in case of accidents.

Making the Blocks and Printing on Fabric

First have the children draw a rough sketch the same size as the block. Encourage them to fill the whole space and to think carefully about which areas of the picture will be cut away on the block. You may discuss the concept of positive and negative space. Once the drawings have been checked by an adult and are satisfactory, the children may copy them onto their Safety-Kut block, first in pencil, then using a permanent marker.

Cutting out the block.

Before printing on the fabric, run test prints on paper using regular printing ink. Ink the blocks with brayers (Speedball). Make additional cuts to clean up the image, repeating the test prints until the definition of the picture is clear (and checked by an adult). This helps prevent wasting the fabric ink or paint on paper, or the use of regular ink on the fabric by mistake. Wipe any residual regular ink off the block with a paper towel before applying the fabric ink. Establish a separate workstation for the final printing on the fabric, preferably supervised. The children who finish their prints first may assist others.

A tray of blocks.

Rolling ink onto the block.

the Safety-Kut block to expose the print. Allow the prints to dry until the next class session before continuing work on them.

Pressing the inked block on the fabric.

Peeling away the fabric.

Prepare the fabric by ironing freezer paper to the back to stabilize it during printing and additional work such as writing and decorating. You may want to determine the arrangement of the fabric blocks in advance by laying them out in the desired format, then labeling them appropriately. This approach worked well for our alphabet quilts, where several colors of fabric were printed. Make sure you have plenty of spare blocks because errors will be made during the printing.

Instruct the children to mark in pencil the position of their print on the right side of the fabric block, by drawing around a print-sized window on a cardboard stencil. Place the inked Safety-Kut block face-down precisely in the pencil square on the fabric. Carefully turn the whole thing over so the freezer paper side is on top. Roll a large, clean, dry brayer firmly and evenly across the print area or rub the area with the palm of your hand. Peel the fabric away from

Finishing Touches

The freezer paper tends to come away from the fabric during printing. If this happens, simply iron it back in place, but beware of wet paint or ink! The children may add color to their dry prints using fabric markers. Encourage them to color in patterns rather than solid areas, to maintain the appearance of a block print, but to enhance and brighten it. Rubber stamp additions, decorations, and writing may also be appropriate. This technique would work well for creating a story quilt with writing and block illustrations.

Three Animal Alliteration Quilts

Supplies

(see page 25 to estimate fabric quantities)
Supplies are the same for all three projects.

* Pale fabric blocks, 6½" x 10½" (17 x 26 cm)
* Bright solid colored fabrics for the frames around the blocks, 1¼" wide (3.5 cm)
* Colorful fabric for sashing, 2½" wide (6 cm), and 2½" square (6 cm) at corners of blocks
* Fabric for binding and backing
* Freezer paper
* Safety-Kut or linoleum cut into 4" square (10 cm) blocks, at least one per child
* Printing supplies: bench hooks, cutting tools and brayers, inking plates
* First aid kit
* Pencils
* Permanent markers
* Regular ink and paper for test prints
* Permanent black fabric ink or black fabric paint for fabric prints
* Rubber stamp pads with regular ink
* Rubber stamp pads with permanent fabric ink
* Rubber stamp alphabet letters
* Fabric markers
* Copies of the block layout, at least one per child
* Batting

Preparation of block layout diagram

To draw the block layout diagram, copy the format from the photographs of the blocks, page 75. Draw the block 6½" x 10½" (17 x 20 cm) and put a margin of ½" (1.5 cm) inside on every side. Children should not write or embellish in this area since it will be eaten up by the seam allowance, or very close to the edge of the block. Draw a 4" square (10 cm) for the block print and a 1" square (2.5 cm) for the letter, then four lines underneath for the alliterative words. Photocopy one for each child.

Each child was assigned a letter of the alphabet. They thought of an animal and three or four descriptive alliterative words starting with their letter. This was particularly challenging for certain letters! The block print illustrated the animal and the alliterative words. Children have wonderful imaginations and they thought up some amusing scenarios, which they reproduced beautifully. For example, "Energetic elephants eat everything," "Vacationing vulture views violet," "Smiling smooth sophisticated slug," "Dirty dog digs deep down," "Pitiful panicking puny pig," and "Ugly unicorns use unicycles!"

The block prints were made following the guidelines already described. Using the block layout handout, the children wrote their alliterative words on the lines provided, in clear legible writing, and practiced rubber stamping their letter in the small box beneath the space for the print image (using a stamp pad with regular ink). After we checked their writing, they took it with their fabric block to the light table and traced the words onto the fabric with colored fabric markers. The letter of the alphabet was rubber stamped in the appropriate position using a fabric ink stamp pad. Care was taken to keep the regular ink and fabric ink stamp pads separate to avoid confusion. Lastly, the children decorated their animal block prints with fabric markers. The children were excited to see the blocks placed on the table as they were completed. In addition to the alphabet blocks, each quilt had a title block and a class identification block.

These projects took eight sessions, which was longer than expected. Two sessions were spent deciding on the animals, alliterative words, and making rough drawings. It took three or four sessions to cut the blocks and another two to print on the fabric, rubber stamp, write the words, and decorate the prints with fabric markers. Some children completed their blocks during the fifth or sixth session and they were drafted to help the others with printing and to supervise the ink station.

Happy Hilarious Animals

70" x 60"
(175 x 150 cm)

There were 29 children in this class, so we made 30 blocks for a layout of 6 x 5. In addition to the 27 alphabet and title blocks, there are three blocks listing all the children's names. The quilting is in silver thread, outlining the fabric blocks, animal prints, and the squares around the rubber stamped letters.

Happy Hilarious Animals.

The children were as happy and hilarious as the finished quilt!

Super Silly Animals   56½" x 69"   (141 x 174 cm)

Super Silly Animals.

The 28 alphabet and title blocks were arranged in a 4 x 7 format. The quilting was done in a variety of colored threads, with the stitches outlining the blocks and prints and making various geometric shapes around the writing.

Absolutely Awesome Animals
4 panels @ 16" x 69"   (40 x 172 cm)

Absolutely Awesome Animals.

The 28 blocks made an alphabet frieze designed to hang around the walls of a classroom. The four panels of 1 x 7 blocks could be hung to suit the configuration of the room. Squiggly-lined quilting stitches surrounded the animal prints, rubber-stamped letters, and the alliterative words. Straight-line quilting outlined the frames on the blocks.

Blocks from Absolutely Awesome Animals.

PROJECTS USING FUSIBLE APPLIQUÉ

Fusible appliqué may be used for a wide range of projects. In simple projects suitable for young children, large shapes such as hands and hearts were cut and fused. Older children can cut any shapes to create pictures. Making intricate images from small snippets will provide a challenge for middle and high school children. Leftover scraps should be saved for snippet projects.

Supplies

Fabric: Choose pale-colored fabric for the background and bright colors for the appliqué pieces to insure that the pictures and shapes are bold and clear.

Fusible webbing: The technique of fusible appliqué relies on commercial adhesive webbing, bonded by heat, to stick appliqué pieces onto a background. For all the 1997 projects, we used Steam-a-Seam 2 and in earlier projects we used Wonder-Under. I prefer Steam-a-Seam 2. Most adhesives require two bonding stages, one to attach the webbing to the appliqué piece, and the other to stick the appliqué piece onto the background. With Steam-a-Seam 2, the bonding is achieved in one stage. The webbing is slightly tacky, so an appliqué piece can be placed in position while other pieces are added. If, before bonding, you need to adjust the position of a piece, simply peel it away from the background and move it. When all the appliqué pieces are correctly arranged, heat bond them by placing a damp cloth over the appliqué and pressing with a hot iron, without moving the iron, for ten seconds. An artist's heat press may be used instead of an iron. Test the settings before fusing the children's work.

Another advantage of Steam-a-Seam 2 is the ease of machine stitching through the layers smoothly, without the machine needle becoming coated in the adhesive. Children may easily blanket stitch by hand around the edge of the appliqué pieces but should not attempt to sew through multiple layers.

Several different fusible products are available. Read and carefully follow the manufacturer's directions. Remember that if the appliqué shape is drawn on the paper backing, when it is cut out the image will be reversed, hence left hands will appear as right hands and vice versa.

In theory, the adhesive will withstand washing and wear and tear. However, we had some problems with Wonder-Under fused appliqué pieces coming away at the edges when the quilts were handled. To prevent this, zigzag machine stitch around the appliqué pieces on the quilt tops or quilt through them for additional stability. Alternatively, hand sew a blanket stitch with embroidery floss to keep the pieces tethered and attractive.

QUILTS WITH HANDS

The hand shape can be used to create a variety of designs. It can be fused onto individual blocks or onto a whole-cloth background or it can be used to make other designs (see page 80).

Cut the fabric, backed with fusible interfacing 6" (16 cm) square. This should be large enough for hands up to nine or ten years old!

To make the hands, ask the children to work in pairs to draw around each other's hands. First practice on rough paper, then draw on the fusible webbing paper (Steam-a-Seam 2 recommended) on the back of the fabric squares.

Cut out the hands with extra care so the piece cut away remains intact. To prevent the Steam-a-Seam 2 paper from shifting while the children are cutting, secure it with pins. Some children are not terribly well coordinated and may need a little additional help with the cutting to prevent fingers from being chopped off! The cut away pieces from the fabric hands may be used in a follow up project for the children to take home.

Carefully cutting the hand shape out of fabric.

Children drawing around each other's hands, first on paper.

Fuse the cut away pieces from the hands onto squares of pale-colored heavier weight fabric and let the children use fabric markers to decorate the hands.

Maggie with the children proudly displaying their decorated hands.

Helping Hands Banner

55" x 44½"   (137 x 113 cm)

Project participants: 24 kindergarten children age 5 and 6, Wilkes School, spring 1994
Minimum recommended age: 5
Level of difficulty: Easy to moderate. Extra volunteers are recommended to help children cut out hands.
Sessions with the children: 1 or 2
Preparation: 2 to 3 hours (cut variety of colored background blocks, add fusible webbing to hand fabric, cut squares)

Supplies
 (see page 25 to estimate fabric quantities)
* Colored background blocks, 9" square (24 cm)
* Variety of contrasting fabrics for hands, 6" square (16 cm)
* Additional fabric for side triangles around edge
* Fabric for border, 2¼" (5.5 cm)
* Fabric for binding and backing
* Fusible webbing (Steam-a-Seam 2 recommended)
* Acrylic paints to embellish hands (in plastic bottles with fine nozzles)
* Batting

Helping Hands Banner.

After the hands were traced, cut out, and fused (see page 78 for instructions), the children embellished them by applying Scribbles paint directly from the bottle nozzles. Most of this was achieved in one class session. We returned for another short session so a few children could complete their painting. The teacher also made a block, and cut out a rabbit shape to fuse for Samson, the class bunny.

The blocks were set on the point and arranged to form a banner that tapered to a point at the bottom. At the sides and top, the points of the blocks were trimmed and small triangles filled in the spaces at the edges. The quilting stitches around each hand accentuated the shapes.

Two other hands quilts (not shown) were made by kindergartners at Wilkes, one in which the blocks were set squarely with narrow sashing strips in-between, and the other, which was a whole-cloth with the hands pointing in a variety of directions. You might like to try one of these alternatives.

TREE QUILTS

Tree quilts are fun to make and may be as simple or complex as you like. Our children wrote woodland words and drew animal pictures, in addition to cutting out the fabric hands for the leaves of the tree.

Supplies for tree quilts.

You may add any of your own variations. For example, make a historical or family tree and include writing in fabric markers on the leaves or on panels around the outside.

Fuse the tree trunk onto the background fabric before the first session. Draw the outline of the trunk on a large piece of butcher paper. Back the bark fabric with fusible interfacing (Steam-a-Seam 2), then place the paper drawing over the top. Cut the trunk out with a rotary cutter, following the outline on the paper, then carefully position it on the background cloth and fuse (see photos).

Fusing the tree trunk with an iron and a pressing cloth.

Cutting out the tree trunk with a rotary cutter.

Placing a cut out hand "leaf" on the background.

Project participants: 4 first grade classes (20 to 21 children in each class) ages 6 and 7, Blakely School, spring 1997
Minimum recommended age: 6
Level of difficulty: Easy to moderate. Extra volunteers recommended to help children cut out hands.

Sessions with the children: 3, optional extra half session for follow-up project (see *Quilts With Hands*, page 78)
Preparation: 3 to 4 hours (cut and fuse tree trunk, cut fabric backed with Steam-a-Seam 2 for hands and words, iron freezer paper onto fabric, cut blocks for animals)

Supplies

(see page 25 to estimate fabric quantities)
Specific background and border sizes are given with each quilt.
* Pale background fabric, 1 yard/meter
* Brown bark fabric, ½ yard/meter
* Variety of colored fabrics for tree leaves (hands), 6" square (16 cm)
* Pale fabric strips for writing woodland words, 2" x 5" (5 x 12 cm)
* Pale fabrics for drawing animals, 5" square (12 cm)

* Fabric for sashing
* Fabric for borders
* Fabric for binding and backing
* Fusible webbing for fusing tree trunk, hands, words, 1½ yards/meters for trunk; 1 yard/meter per 8 children for 8 hands and 8 words with extra for errors
* Freezer paper for stabilizing animal blocks
* Scissors (suitable for children to cut fabric)
* Fabric markers
* Batting

Our projects took three sessions. In Session I the hands were traced and cut and placed on the tree branches by the children. Then we discussed words describing trees, including the bark texture, and wrote them on the board. The children practiced writing a word of their choice four times on strips of paper. In Session II they wrote their words on fabric strips (after the practice writing had been checked by an adult), then started drawing a woodland animal, first on a sheet of paper, then on the freezer paper side of the animal block. A light table was used for the children to trace the outline of the animals onto the fabric side of the block with a black fabric marker (see page 39). Session III was spent finishing the tracing of the animals and coloring them with fabric markers.

We made each of our four tree quilts with slightly different arrangements of the animals and words. The children were excited to see the completed quilt tops and loved pointing out their hands, words, and animals.

Tracing an animal at the light table.

One of the border blocks for Tree of Life.

Tree of Life
54" x 52½"
(135 x 131 cm)

Tree of Life.

The tree words were fused to the tree trunk and the animal blocks were evenly spaced around three sides of the quilt. The central yellow panel was made from one yard/meter of fabric trimmed to 41½" x 34½" (104 x 86 cm) after the fusing was finished. The outer border strips were cut 3½" (9 cm) wide. Rays of sun and large leaves were quilted on the yellow background.

Woodland Walk 58" x 52"   (145 x 130 cm)

Woodland Walk.

The tree words were fused to the tree trunk and the ground on each side of the trunk. The blue central panel was a one yard/meter piece trimmed to 41½" x 36" (104 x 90 cm) after the fusing was completed. Steam-a-Seam 2 was added to the animal blocks and they were fused to the border, cut 9" (24 cm) wide. A curly-edged cutter was used to trim the animal blocks before they were fused. The quilted clouds added to the charm of this quilt.

Proudly displaying the finished quilt.

Forest Fantasy
50½" x 42½"   (126 x 106 cm)

Forest Fantasy.

Steam-a-Seam 2 was added to the animals and they were cut out and fused to the tree. The words were cut into leaf shapes before being fused to the green border, cut 4½" (11 cm) wide. The peach-colored central panel was a one yard/meter piece trimmed to 35" x 42½" (88 x 106 cm) after the fusing. The background was quilted with a crosshatch and the border had a silver zigzag stitch weaving between the leaves. Silver zigzag stitching was also used to secure the binding, which added a decorative touch.

Friendship Tree
53" x 47"   (133 x 117 cm)

Friendship Tree.

For the *Friendship Tree* quilt, animals and word blocks were alternated in the border and distributed evenly around the central panel. The green central panel was a one-yard/meter piece trimmed to 34½" x 41" (86 x 102 cm)

after the fusing was completed. The bark of the tree was stipple quilted and the green background was echo quilted around the tree outline.

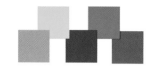

Hearts, like hands, may be used in a variety of ways. Use your imagination and be creative! You may embellish your hearts with paint, ribbons, and beads. Large fused hearts look pretty with embroidery stitches added. Blanket stitch works well for the outline. For examples of hand sewn heart quilt blocks, see pages 91-102.

I was overcome when I was presented with this beautiful quilt at a special assembly where all the Blakely children shared their quilts. Every participant from the 14 quilt project classes cut out a small fabric heart backed with Steam-a-Seam 2 and signed it. The hearts were fused to the pieced quilt top. They formed a heart wreath in the center and radiated out from the middle, with more scattered in the pretty pansy border. The crosshatch quilting of a large heart in the middle accentuated the heart shape, and quilting stitches linked all the little hearts together. This quilt will always bring back my fond memories of being part of the Blakely family for five months.

Heartfelt Thanks
51½" x 51½" (129 x 129 cm)

Heartfelt Thanks.

Project participants: 350+ children ages 6 to 11, first through fifth grade classes at Blakely School, spring 1997
Minimum recommended age: 6, good project for large numbers and mixed ages
Level of difficulty: Easy

Sessions with the children: 10 to 20 minutes with each group
Preparation: 2 to 3 hours (add Steam-a-Seam 2 to heart fabric, cut squares)

Supplies
(see page 25 to estimate fabric quantities)
* Pale fabric for the center square:
    1 piece 36½" x 36½" (91.5 x 91.5 cm)
    or 9 pieces 12½" square (31.5cm)
* Framing strips, 2½" wide (6 cm)
* Selection of red, pink, and coral squares for hearts, 2" square (5 cm), at least one per child
* Fabric for border, 1 yard/meter, 6½" wide (16.5 cm)

* Corner 9-patches, made from 2½" squares (6.5 cm) or corner squares, 6½" square (16.5 cm)
* Fabric for binding and backing
* Fusible webbing (Steam-a-Seam 2 recommended) to bond hearts
* Permanent silver pen or fabric marker (should be clearly visible on hearts)
* Batting

DRAGONS AND CASTLES ON QUILTS

Children love folk tales about medieval times and they will enjoy letting their imaginations run wild while they draw castles, dragons, and nobility. You may use the children's drawings as patterns for the fusible appliqué, or provide the children with fabric backed with fusible web-

bing so they can cut their own shapes. Younger children can make nobility out of pre-cut figures and clothing, pick out yarn for the hair, and ribbon and beads etc. as embellishments.

Medieval Memories
75" x 75"   (187 x 187 cm)

Medieval Memories.

Project participants: 90 children ages 5 to 10, kindergarten through fourth grade, The Island School, spring 1997. Two quilts were made.
Minimum recommended age: 5, good project for mixed age group
Level of difficulty: Easy to moderate

Sessions with the children: 1 or 2 with each class
Preparation: 2 to 3 hours (cut out bodies and clothing of nobility, collect suitable extras such as yarn etc. for embellishments, gather selection of fabrics for appliqué)

Supplies
 (see page 25 to estimate fabric quantities)
Prepare the quantity needed for number of children.
* White or pale blocks for dragons and castles, 12" square (32 cm)
* White or pale rectangles for shields and nobility, 12" x 6¼" (32 x 16.75 cm)
* Variety of fabric scraps for the appliqué (not necessarily 100% cotton)
* Fabric for sashing
* Fabric for borders
* Fabric for binding and backing
* Fusible webbing (Steam-a-Seam 2 recommended)
* Yarn, buttons, lace, cord, sequins, braid, etc. for embellishing
* Batting

Two of the rectangular blocks for nobility and shields make a block the same size as the dragon and castle blocks. Bear this in mind when planning your quilt, and try to use a number of blocks that will fit together easily. If extra blocks are needed you will have no trouble finding children eager to help make more.

Each class designed different parts of the quilt in the medieval theme: kindergarten - princes and princesses; first grade - castles; second grade - shields; third grade - a variety; fourth grade - dragons.

For the princes and princesses, the kindergartners were provided with pre-cut bodies, outfits, and embellish-

ing materials. The children in the other classes drew their designs on paper and were given a variety of fabric scraps from which to choose. Adult volunteers transferred the paper drawings to the chosen fabrics and fused the pieces with Wonder-Under. The shapes were also stitched down to prevent the adhesive from peeling. The sashing strips between the blocks helped the pictures look distinctive and the borders provided an attractive finish. The quilt was stipple quilted, which also enhanced the children's images.

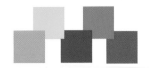

SNIPPET PROJECTS

This technique uses adhesive webbing to bond appliqué pieces to a whole-cloth background. There are many project possibilities, ranging from the simple - where large pieces are bonded - to the complex - involving small snippets of fabric. See page 77 for information on adhesives (Steam-a-Seam 2 recommended). The children will enjoy building pictures and you will be excited by their creativity. For excellent instructions on this technique and more project ideas, refer to Cindy Walter's book *Snippet Sensations*.

The quilts shown illustrate how small pieces (snippets) can be cut and fused to make composite pictures or collages. This is a wonderful way to use leftover scraps in a creative way.

Water World.

Water World
32" x 25"
(81 x 62 cm)

Project participant:
Bobby Henry,
age 10, 1996

Bobby made this delightful underwater scene using left over scraps from one of Marilyn Doheny's projects.

Grassickett 36" x 45"   (90 x 112 cm)

Grassickett.

Project participant: Brielyn Doheny, age 16, 1997

Menorah 56" x 36"   (140 x 90 cm)

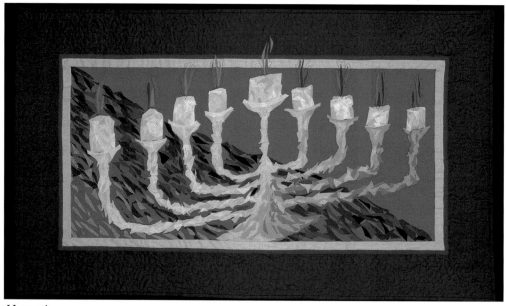

Menorah.

Older children will enjoy designing more complicated compositions such as these two beautiful examples.

Hand sewing is time-consuming, both to prepare the materials and to teach, but extremely rewarding, and you will find that the children take great pride in their work. Enlist extra volunteers to help, and aim for a minimum ratio of one adult per six children. The more individual attention you can provide when the children are learning to sew, the better, and the fewer the frustrations of tangled thread and unthreaded needles. Make sure the adults know what they are doing! It is important that the children are all taught in the same way, so train your volunteers to pin and sew correctly.

Hand sewing projects are recommended for children eight years or older. Younger children can be taught to sew, but are much slower and have more problems with threading needles and tangling the thread. Older children will be faster at learning and have better manual dexterity. The ideal age range is ten to 14. All hand sewn projects are challenging, but fun too, and the children will enjoy seeing their projects progress.

For a school project, keep all the work in progress in the classroom. Some will disappear if you allow the children to take it home.

Children love to master hand sewing.

The children will master the sewing quickly if they are given individual attention and encouragement. Once they know the basic stitches and understand what they are doing, they will happily sit sewing and chatting to one another. If they become restless or distracted after 30 to 45 minutes, give them a break.

Involve the children in as many of the quilt making stages as possible. Set a deadline or incentive to finish, and suggest some goals. If possible, display the work in a public place so it can be admired and the children receive the praise they deserve.

Refer to pages 16-24 for instructions in the basic stitches, preparation, piecing, appliqué, embroidery, and quilting.

Everyone likes making heart blocks.

HEART AND 4-PATCH QUILTS

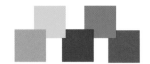

Both piecing and embroidery are used to make the blocks for these heart and 4-patch quilts. The blocks are small (finished size 6", 16 cm), and they can be sewn in two or three sessions. This is a great way to introduce children to these sewing skills without swamping them with an overwhelming project. Our children made one of each kind of block, and over half of them finished both blocks in four sessions.

Heart and 4-patch blocks in progress, and supplies.

Brave Heart 42" x 42"   (105 x 105 cm)

Brave Heart.

Dragon Heart
49" x 49"   (124 x 124 cm)

Dragon Heart.

Project participants: 48 children (24 on each quilt) ages 6 to 10, The Family Classroom, spring 1997
Minimum recommended age: 8
Level of difficulty: Moderate to challenging
Sessions with the children: 4 to 6 (add 5 sessions for hand quilting)

Preparation: 3 to 4 hours per quilt (4-patches: cut squares, mark stitching lines using plastic template; hearts: cut background squares, back heart fabric with Steam-a-Seam 2, cut squares, wind embroidery floss onto cardboard tags to reduce tangling)

Supplies
(see page 25 to estimate fabric quantities)
* Pale fabric for 4-patches, 3½" square (9.5 cm), 2 per block
* Bright contrasting fabric for 4-patches, 3½" square (9.5 cm), 2 per block
* Muslin or white fabric for heart backgrounds, 6½" square (17.5 cm)
* Fabric for border if desired, *Dragon Heart*, 3½" wide (9.5 cm)
* For hand quilting - quilting frame, quilting needles (size 7), quilting thread, thimbles to fit children
* Fabric for binding and backing

* Template plastic (trace the inner dotted line on Template H, Appendix 6, and cut it out)
* Paper on which to pin the children's work (at least 8" square, 20 cm)
* Embroidery needles, sizes 3 to 9
* Pins
* Thread (mercerized cotton covered polyester)
* Contrasting fabric for hearts, 5" squares (12 cm)
* Fusible webbing for hearts (Steam-a-Seam 2 recommended)
* Cardboard heart templates (see Appendix 6)
* Embroidery floss
* Batting

Sessions I and II were spent sewing the 4-patch blocks together. The children chose their two light and two contrasting squares, pinned them to a sheet of paper in the correct layout, then began stitching. In Session III, children who had finished their 4-patch block started their heart block. By Session IV, all the children were working on the hearts. They chose their heart fabric, drew around a cardboard heart template on the Steam-a-Seam 2 paper on the back, then cut out the heart. The hearts were fused to the pale background blocks. Next the children embroidered in blanket stitch around the edge of the heart and, if time allowed, they could make more embroidery stitches in the middle of the heart to decorate it.

Blanket stitching around the heart.

Showing off the 4-patches.

Tying Brave Heart.

Hand quilting Brave Heart.

In *Dragon Heart*, the multicolored 4-patch and heart blocks were arranged alternately, and there was a border. The quilt was machine quilted around the hearts and with diagonal lines through the 4-patches.

In the red and white *Brave Heart*, the 25 heart blocks were grouped together in the center, and the 4-patch blocks made a border around the outside. The quilt was machine quilted in the ditch around each block. Five more sessions were spent with the children, tying each 4-patch block with red embroidery floss and hand quilting around each heart.

CRAZY PATCHWORK HEARTS

These delightful heart blocks took patience and determination to make, but the children rose to the challenge and were thrilled when the time came to select charms and buttons to complete their work. By then they were sewing and threading needles with ease.

The crazy patchwork pieces were hand-stitched together. The heart was made using a reverse fusible appliqué technique. A block with a heart hole cut in it was fused to the patchwork piece, then the heart outline and seam lines were decorated with three or four different embroidery stitches. We cheered as each of our blocks was finished, and as our deadline approached, the children

helped each other. Congratulations were definitely in order, and the sense of achievement for this difficult project was tremendous.

Before you begin, tell the children about Victorian crazy quilts. Show them examples of the elaborate embroidery and odd-shaped patchwork pieces that were used (show pictures or if you have a quilt, bring it to share). We made four quilts, three large and one small, from our 78 blocks. The methods and supplies were the same for all the quilts. Details of sashing, border sizes, and layout are listed with each quilt. Refer to pages 16-21 for instructions in hand piecing and embroidery.

Starting with the red triangle, strips were added, the heart background fused, and the block was embroidered.

Project participants: 3 third grade classes (78 children) ages 8 and 9, Blakely School, spring 1997
Minimum recommended age: 8
Level of difficulty: Challenging
Sessions with the children: 8 to 12 (older children will sew faster)
Preparation: 3 to 4 hours per class, 1 to 2 hours for individual or small projects (gather scraps for crazy patchwork, cut Steam-a-Seam 2 squares, cut background fabric blocks, add Steam-a-Seam 2 squares, cut out hearts, wind embroidery floss onto cardboard)

Supplies
(see page 25 to estimate fabric quantities)
* Red fabric triangles, 5" square (12 cm) cut in half diagonally - minimum of 1 triangle per block
* Fabric scraps in a variety of medium to dark colors, 2" x 4" (5 x 10 cm) or larger - 4 per block
* Fabric strips for practicing sewing, 2" x 6" (5 x 15 cm) - 2 per child
* Fabric for sashing
* Fabric for border
* Dark gray fabric to place between quilt top and batting
* Fabric for binding and backing
* Thread
* Embroidery needles, sizes 3 to 9
* Pins
* Pincushions
* Rulers and pencils for children to mark the stitching lines
* Pale fabric blocks, 8½" square (22 cm)
* Fusible webbing (Steam-a-Seam 2 recommended), 7" square (18 cm)
* Cardboard half-heart template (see Appendix 6)
* Embroidery floss
* Charms, 2 per child
* Buttons, 1 per child
* Batting

Preparation of Block Background

Cut 8½" (22 cm) squares of pale background fabric. Cut 7" (18 cm) squares of Steam-a-Seam 2 and add a square to the center of the wrong side of each block. Fold the blocks in half with the Steam-a-Seam 2 paper on the outside.

Place the cardboard half-heart template so the straight edge is along the fold in the block and the tip is approximately 1½" (4 cm) from the bottom edge of the block. Draw around it in pencil. Pin the free edges of the block to prevent it from slipping as you cut. Cut along the pencil line using sharp fabric cutting scissors. Unfold the block to reveal the heart-shaped hole cut out of the center.

Working With the Children

This project took much longer than we anticipated. At the start, M.J. and I were the only adults. We quickly asked for extra help from volunteers, which made a huge difference. Some children mastered the sewing quickly and moved along at a steady pace. Others were stuck on one seam line for a whole session unless an adult monitored their progress frequently. Children who finished quickly were asked to help others. Be prepared to be flexible and give extra attention to those children falling behind.

Demonstrate the basic sewing stitch (three running stitches, then a backstitch) at the start of each session to remind the children. By the time you reach the embroidery part, you will probably have children at several different stages. Demonstrate the blanket stitch each time to all the children and work with small groups to teach the other stitches. Older children will be faster. Follow the block progression in the photograph on page 96.

Session I: Learn the basic stitches on the practice strips.
Session II: Continue practicing. Select fabrics for the heart block. Start sewing scraps onto the triangle.
Sessions III, IV, V: Continue sewing crazy patchwork. Position the background block with the cutout heart so no raw edges of patchwork are exposed, and fuse.
Session VI: Learn the blanket stitch and embroider around the outside of the heart.
Session VII: Continue the blanket stitch. Learn cross stitch and embroider along one or two seam lines.
Session VIII: Learn the chain stitch and embroider along one or two seams.
Session IX: Learn the laced running stitch and stitch the last seam. Use metallic thread!
Session X: Select two charms and a button. Sew them onto the block to finish. Congratulations!

Give the children some practice fabric strips to teach them the basics of tying a knot and sewing running and backstitches (see page 17 for basic stitch instructions). Once they have mastered marking the seam allowance in pencil and the basic stitching on their practice pieces, allow them to select the fabric for their crazy heart (a red triangle and four fabric scraps).

Marking the seam allowance.

Sewing the first strip onto the red triangle.

Sew the pieces together like the practice strips, marking the seam allowance on one piece and lining up the raw edges and pinning, then sewing.

Sew one strip on each side of the triangle. After each strip is sewn, an adult should press the patchwork with the seam allowances on the back ironed away from the triangle. The fourth scrap may be added on any side.

Lay and turn a background block (with a heart hole) on top of the patchwork to help determine the best position. In some cases the patchwork piece is already big enough without adding the fourth scrap. When the piecing is complete, let the children manipulate the background block until the heart hole is in the desired position. There should be no raw edges of fabric visible through the heart hole.

To fuse the block use a hot iron and damp pressing cloth or a heat press. For ironing, place a piece of nonstick paper (from the Steam-a-Seam 2) between the wrong side of the block and the ironing board. Use a damp cloth over

Selecting fabric strips.

At the end of each session, ask the children to stack all their patchwork pieces. Write their name on the practice piece and put this on to the top of the stack, then pin the whole lot together.

Maggie watches as the second strip is attached to the red triangle.

the top of the block and press, holding the iron still for ten seconds to fuse. We used a heat press set at 350°F and pressed the blocks for 30 seconds. If you use a press, test the settings before you try it on the children's work and place the block between two pieces of nonstick paper in the press. The nonstick paper is used for both ironing and pressing because there may be some areas of the Steam-a-Seam 2 exposed on the back of the block with no patchwork on which to fuse. The paper prevents the mess of having these parts becoming fused to the ironing board or the base of the press.

After fusing, allow the block to cool and trim away the excess patchwork fabric on the back around the fused area. Now the work is all in one piece (except for the practice piece, which the children can take home). Stick a name label on the wrong side in a corner away from the edge of the heart.

The children were delighted with their fused heart blocks and eager to start the embroidery. Teach the blanket

Blanket stitching around the heart.

stitch first and outline the hearts, stitching along the very edge of the heart hole. Use a variety of stitches (cross stitch, chain stitch, laced running stitch) for the seam lines inside the heart (see page 20 for instructions). After the blanket stitch, the children should have no trouble with the other stitches and progress will be faster. We had some gold and silver embroidery floss that the children were eager to use, but we found that it frayed and tangled rather easily when pulled through the fabric. However, they had no problems using it for the laced running stitch where it was passed in and out of running stitches on the surface and not pulled through the fabric. This decorative stitch was simple to execute and the children enjoyed the chance to use the metallic floss.

The reward for finishing the embroidery was to select two gold charms and a button! These could be sewn anywhere on the heart to complete the block. The children were extremely proud of their work. This was a difficult project and they deserved high praise and congratulations. The commitment and perseverance of our eight and nine year old children impressed us. They worked hard, had fun, and quite justifiably felt proud of their efforts.

When the quilt tops were pieced, we noticed a shadow effect of the fused edges of fabric showing through the blocks. To reduce this, we inserted a dark gray piece of fabric between the pieced top and the batting. This made the quilts heavier, but successfully disguised the shadow effect and improved the appearance.

The Steam-a-Seam 2 backed hearts that had been cut out of the blocks were used in a follow-up project for the children to take home. M.J. scanned the completed heart blocks into the computer, then printed images of them on special transfer paper. The image was transferred onto the fabric heart, then fused onto a square block of contrasting fabric. The children were pleased to have a memento from the project to remind them of their beautiful quilt blocks and all their hard work.

Proudly displaying a heart block before starting to embroider.

Hearts Together
52" x 52"
(105 x 105 cm)

Hearts Together.

Holiday Hearts
52" x 52"   (130 x 130 cm)

Holiday Hearts.

Both of these quilts had 25 blocks set in a 5 x 5 configuration. The sashing strips were cut 2½" (6 cm) wide with 2½" (6 cm) squares at the intersections. *Holiday Hearts* had an outer border cut 3" (8 cm) wide with no squares at the intersections. Both quilts were quilted with a serpentine stitch along the block edges and a scalloped stitch around the hearts.

Crazy Hearts
58½" x 40"   (146 x 100 cm)

Crazy Hearts.

This quilt had 24 blocks in a 4 x 6 configuration. The fuchsia-colored sashing strips were cut 2½" (6 cm) wide with 2½" (6 cm) black squares at the intersections. The quilt was machine quilted with a straight stitch around each heart and the children tied the center of each black square with embroidery floss.

4-Patch Hearts
26" x 26" (65 x 65 cm)

4-Patch Hearts.

This quilt was made from four blocks. Each block was framed with a narrow red strip cut 1" (2.5cm) wide. The sashing strips were cut 3" (8 cm) wide, with 3" (8 cm) squares at the intersections. It was quilted with serpentine and straight stitches around the blocks and a scallop stitch around each heart.

Since this is a demanding project, I recommend that children make only one block unless they are really diligent or use the sewing machine to piece the patchwork. We don't want sewing burnout! A single block with sashing added would make a charming small wall hanging or pillow cover (what a great gift for Grandma), or small groups may combine their blocks to make a larger quilt.

TRADITIONAL PATCHWORK BLOCKS

See Appendices 1 to 6 for block diagrams, piecing instructions, and templates for more than 25 traditional quilt blocks, 9" square (24 cm). Appendix 1 shows several traditional blocks. The simplest are the 4-patch and 9-patch designs. Some blocks, such as Log Cabin and Ohio Star, are more challenging. There are two appliqué blocks - a heart and Sunbonnet Sue. You may want to limit the children's choice to six or seven blocks to simplify the project and use fewer templates.

Metric template sizes are provided in Appendix 2, but for hand piecing, where the seam allowance size is not critical, you may use the templates in Appendix 6.

Trace the inner dotted lines to make templates for hand piecing. Children 11 and older can easily draw around the templates under your guidance and cut out their own patchwork pieces. For patchwork, small scraps of fabric may be used, or purchase a variety of light, medium, and dark "fat quarters." Encourage the children to share and exchange fabrics.

All the blocks in Appendix 1 are included in the quilt shown, *Color Wheel Sampler*, 71" x 60" (178 x 150 cm), made in 1998.

I made this sampler to illustrate the different blocks and to teach the children some color theory. The blocks, arranged around the color wheel in the center, were made from primary and secondary colored fabrics in different combinations with black and white. The 9-patch and bow-tie blocks were repeated with the colors reversed to show how different color placement can change the appearance dramatically. The quilt was machine quilted with many different quilting patterns using both straight-line and free-motion quilting, and the block names were hand embroidered. (Note: all the block patterns except for the color wheel block are included in this book.)

See page 17 for teaching the basic sewing techniques and preparing the materials for the blocks. See page 19 for instructions for the appliqué blocks (Sunbonnet Sue and heart). The preparation is time-consuming (20 to 30 minutes per block). Preparing all the block packages is a huge job for one person. Organize a work party with your volunteers and have fun! Children 11 years or older can help draw around the templates and cut their own patchwork pieces. Recruit volunteers to help teach the children how to sew (the more the better) and train them so everyone does it the same way. The energy and enthusiasm of the children will reward you for all your hard work, and of course, they will complete a beautiful quilt.

Color Wheel Sampler.

Pioneer Patchwork
81½" x 67"
(204 x 168 cm)

Project participants: 26 fifth grade children ages 10 and 11, Wilkes School, spring 1994
Minimum recommended age: 8
Level of difficulty: Challenging, additional volunteers needed
Sessions with the children: 4 to 6
Preparation: 20 to 30 minutes per block and ½ hour training session for volunteer helpers (make plastic templates, make block packages)

Supplies
(see page 25 to estimate fabric quantities)
* Variety of fabrics for patchwork blocks
* Calico strips for framing blocks, 2¾" wide (7 cm)
* Fabric for binding and backing
* Template plastic (trace the dotted lines and cut templates from Appendix 6 and use template guide in Appendix 2)
* Sandpaper to keep fabric from shifting while drawing round templates
* Paper for pinning children's blocks, approx. 15" square (36 cm)
* Pins
* Pincushions
* Embroidery needles, sizes 3 to 9
* Thread
* Batting

Pioneer Patchwork.

Ask the children to choose a block pattern from Appendix 1 and to specify their color preferences. My friend and fellow-coordinator Wendy Simon had a wonderful stash of old calico prints, which she generously shared, and the children brought scraps of cotton fabric from home. We used these to prepare the block packages.

Train as many volunteers as possible to help teach the children to hand sew. We had six, and each one worked with a group of four or five children who were all making similar quilt blocks. In Session I, tell the children to pin out the patchwork block pieces on paper and teach them how to pin accurately and sew with running and back-stitches (see page 18). Explain the piecing order (see Appendices 3 to 5). In the remaining sessions the volunteers should continue to work with small groups of chil-

dren. The children need help when sewing across seam intersections and should be reminded of the correct piecing order. Our children were also given time to sew while the teacher read out loud, when they had completed an assignment, and during rainy day recesses. Our blocks were completed over a period of about three weeks.

We added calico strips to frame each block, then trimmed them evenly on each side so all the blocks measured 13½" square (35 cm) before we joined them together. We made four additional blocks and the children arranged the 30 blocks in a 5 x 6 format. The quilt was machine quilted with a serpentine stitch. The children were so proud of their work and excited to see all the blocks together in one big quilt.

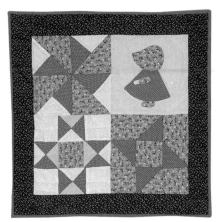

4-Block Patchwork Samplers
23" x 23"
(58 x 58 cm)

4-Block Patchwork Samplers.

Project participants: 12 children ages 8 to 11, Wilkes School extra-curricular program, spring 1995
Minimum recommended age: 8, ideally 10 or older
Level of difficulty: Challenging
Sessions with the children: Minimum of 6, preferably 8, 1 to 2 hours

Preparation: 1 hour (trace and cut plastic templates) Additional 20 to 30 minutes to prepare each block package (children 11 or older can prepare their own materials). Before the first session, provide the children with a list of supplies (you could organize a field trip).

Supplies
(see page 25 to estimate fabric quantities)
* Sewing supplies - pins, neutral colored thread, embroidery needles sizes 3 to 9, fabric scissors
* Quilting supplies - needles size 7 to 9, quilting thread, 14" embroidery hoop, thimble (that fits!)
* 4 or 5 different fabric pieces for blocks - light, medium, and dark
* Pale fabric for appliqué background, 10" square (27 cm)
* ½ yard/meter fabric for sashing, 2½" wide (6 cm)
* Fabric for border, 3" wide (8 cm)

* ¾ yard/meter fabric for backing
* ¼ yard/meter fabric for binding
* Paper for pinning out blocks, approx. 15" square (35 cm)
* Template plastic (trace dotted lines and cut templates from Appendix 6 and use the template guide in Appendix 2)
* Sandpaper to keep fabric from shifting while drawing around templates
* Masking tape or T-pins for basting
* Batting - large package divided among children

Wendy and I taught this project as a beginning quilting class to a group of 12 children. We only had four two-hour sessions, each one month apart, which was not enough time for each child to piece four blocks and hand quilt their quilt. We prepared all the block packages for the children and spent several lunch hours offering additional help for sewing. The children did a lot of homework to stay on target. Most of them rose to the challenge and we had a delightful display of their completed quilts in the school library. I recommend eight one- to two-hour sessions.

Hand quilting.

Encourage the children to use well-fitting thimbles (metal or leather) when hand quilting.

Working With the Children

Begin by talking about quilts and the sampler project. Bring books for the children to see and tell them about different kinds of quilts and techniques. Encourage them to talk about quilts they have seen outside the class and to bring quilts from home to share. Let the children choose four block patterns from Appendix 1. You may like to simplify the choice by limiting it to only seven or eight blocks. Check the supplies the children have brought and make sure everyone has what they need. Discuss which fabrics to use where.

For the next four sessions, have the children complete one block per session. They will have time to draw around the plastic templates, cut their own fabric, and do some stitching in class. For children younger than 11, prepare their block packages. For Sunbonnet Sue or the appliqué heart, prepare the appliqué pieces for the children (see page 19) or have the children cut the pieces with fusible webbing, bond them, and blanket stitch around the edges. They may finish each block at home before the next session. Gather up the completed blocks and machine piece them for the children before the next session. Older children can be taught to machine piece for themselves, but you'll need to add another one or two sessions for this.

At the sixth meeting, let the children do the basting (page 32). Encourage them to help each other and work in pairs. Start hand quilting if there is time (page 22).

The hand quilting can be done in the next session and at home. Take a sewing machine to class and machine stitch as many bindings as possible or roll the backing to the front instead of adding a binding.

The final session can be spent finishing the hand quilting and hand sewing the binding to the back. Take fabric markers and freezer paper to class so the children can make labels to sew on the back of their quilts. The children will probably need more time to complete their hand quilting, but they may do this after the binding has been added.

This is a difficult project. Show the children how much you appreciate all their hard work. You could have a party to celebrate the completion of the quilts!

Children proudly show their completed quilts.

This project can easily be scaled down. A small group quilt, with each child piecing just one or two blocks instead of four, is a possibility. Alternatively, the children could each make a little wall hanging or a patchwork pillow from only one block (see patchwork pillows on page 107).

Patchwork Pillows.

Patchwork Pillows

12" x 16" and 14" x 14" (metric, see below)

Project participants: 6 children age 14, spring 1997
Minimum recommended age: 10, or 8 if an adult does the machine sewing
Level of difficulty: Moderate to challenging

Sessions with the children: 2 or 3, 2 to 3 hours each
Preparation: 1 hour (trace and cut plastic templates)
Additional 20 to 30 minutes to prepare each block package if the children are not old enough to do it.

Supplies
(see page 25 to estimate fabric quantities)
* Basic sewing supplies - pins, neutral colored thread, embroidery needles sizes 3 to 9, fabric scissors
* Paper for pinning out blocks, 15" square (35 cm)
* Sandpaper to keep fabric from shifting while drawing around templates
* Template plastic (trace dotted lines cut templates from Appendix 6 and use the template guide in Appendix 2)

* Pillow form, 12" x 16" or 14" x 14", for 9" (24 cm) block with border
* 3 or 4 different fabrics for blocks
* ¼ yard/meter fabric for border (adjust size of strips to fit pillow form)
* ½ yard/meter fabric for backing
* Optional: fabric for framing block, 1" strips (2.5 cm)

If using metric measurements, adjust the border sizes to fit the metric pillow form. This project required hand and machine sewing (see page 16). The traditional 9" (24 cm) blocks were sewn by hand, then the borders and backing were added by machine.

For the border allow for ½" (1.5 cm) seam allowances around the outer edges of the top. For example, an unfinished top measuring 15" x 15" (39 x 39 cm) will fit a 14" x 14" (36 x 36 cm) pillow form. For the back, cut two pieces large enough to overlap by a minimum of 2½" (6 cm) on the back, creating an envelope for the pillow form. For example, for a pillow form 14" x 14" (36 x 36 cm), cut the pieces 15" x 11" (38 x 27 cm) and 15" x 9" (38 x 24 cm). This allows for a ½" (1 cm) seam allowance around the outside and 1" (2.5 cm) to turn under the raw edges in the middle of the pillow back.

Fold the middle edge of each back piece over twice and hem or machine stitch the fold in place. Place the patchwork piece right side up on the table. Lay the backing pieces over it with the wrong sides on top. Line them up with the outside edges of the pieced top. They should overlap in the middle by at least 2½" (6 cm). Pin them in place and machine stitch around the edge with a ½" (1 cm) seam allowance. Turn the right sides out and insert the pillow form. Alternatively, make the back with a zipper or snaps.

Place right sides of pillow front and backs together.

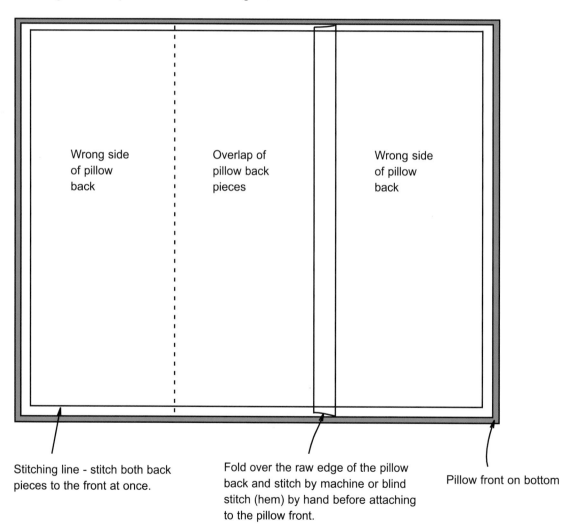

Wrong side of pillow back

Overlap of pillow back pieces

Wrong side of pillow back

Stitching line - stitch both back pieces to the front at once.

Fold over the raw edge of the pillow back and stitch by machine or blind stitch (hem) by hand before attaching to the pillow front.

Pillow front on bottom

During the first session, concentrate on hand sewing the traditional block, then in the second session machine sew the borders and the back of the pillow cover. You may need a third session to complete the project. See Appendices 1 to 6 for patterns, templates, and piecing instructions. To simplify choosing block patterns and the number of templates used, limit the children's choice to six or seven of the blocks.

The 14-year-old Camp Fire Girls who did this project were much easier to teach to sew than the younger eight to 11 year-olds who made the four block samplers on page 105. They drew around the plastic templates and cut out their own patchwork pieces. They had no trouble threading needles and keeping them threaded, and the ease and rapidity of their sewing surprised me.

Cutting out pieces.

Initially the children were apprehensive about using the sewing machine, but they soon became more confident and relaxed. First they practiced sewing straight lines on graph paper with a ¼" seam allowance. I showed them how to use a rotary cutter and supervised them while they cut the border strips and backing pieces for the pillow cover. They sewed their border strips to the blocks and attached the back pieces using the machine. Of course, there was much excitement when the pillow forms were stuffed inside, and the pillows were tossed about amidst giggles and shrieks of delight!

Drawing around a template.

Using a sewing machine, children are able to piece lap quilts in a relatively short time. There are many simple designs that work well for beginners. Children 12 or older should be able to use a rotary cutter (with supervision) and learn fast-piecing techniques (see page 14). For instructions to teach machine sewing, see page 21.

After some practice machine stitching on graph paper, the children become confident and eager to sew on fabric. A good way to start is to cut up an assortment of 4" (10 cm) or larger squares of fabric which may be arranged and assembled by machine into a doll or lap quilt. This will give the children practice at making a consistent ¼" (0.75 cm) seam allowance without complicated piecing. Then they may progress to more intricate designs. Appendices 1 to 6 provide block diagrams, templates, and piecing instructions for traditional quilt blocks. Use the outer solid line on the templates in Appendix 6. To draft metric templates, use the measurements provided in Appendix 2 and add 0.75 cm seam allowances to each side.

4-Patch Quilts 52" x 42"   (130 x 105 cm)

4-Patch Quilts.

Project participants: 10 Girl Scouts ages 12 to 16, 1996
Minimum recommended age: 10, 12 for rotary cutting
Level of difficulty: Moderate to challenging

Sessions with the children: Minimum of 4, 1½ to 2 hours
Preparation: Students do it all! The ideal adult to child ratio is 3:1.

Supplies
* Variety of 5 or more ⅛ or ¼ yard/meter fabric pieces, or one ⅔ yard/meter piece
* 1½ yards/meters fabric for background
* 1¾ yards/meters fabric for backing (make sure it matches or coordinates with border since it will be rolled to front to make binding)

* Optional: ½ yard/meter fabric for binding (used only if separate binding is added)
* Sewing machine in good working order
* Rotary cutter and mat
* Basic sewing supplies
* Batting
* Pearl cotton or embroidery floss for tying

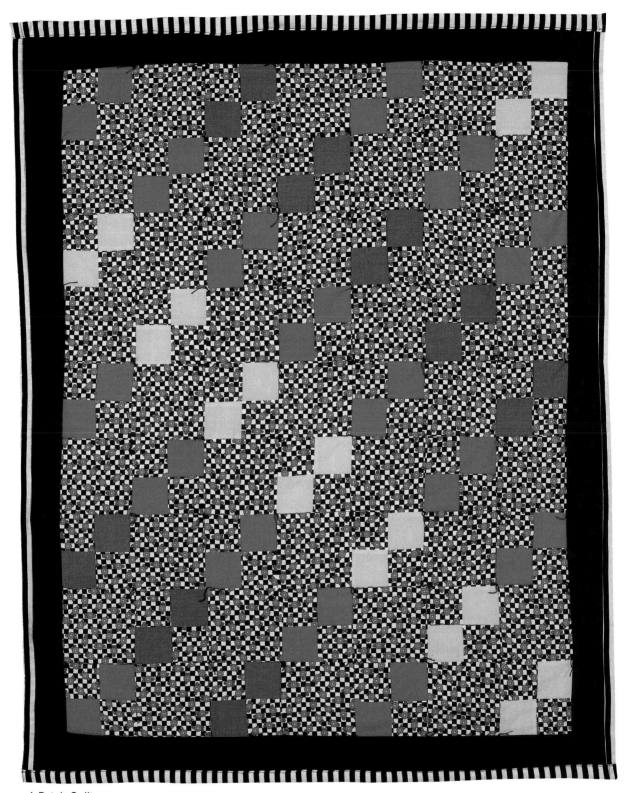

4-Patch Quilt.

Pattern by Margaret Mathisson. The girls each made their own 4-patch quilt with such success that some went on to more complicated patterns like the Log Cabin. They began with an exciting shopping trip to select their fabrics.

The first sewing session was a whole day, with the girls coming and going as their schedules allowed, then they met four more times

Proudly displaying the finished quilts.

Become familiar with threading and using the sewing machine and practice accurate ¼" (0.75 cm) seam allowances.

Rotary cut the fabric for the 4-patches. Cut the ¼ yard/meter pieces in half at the fold, making pieces 9" x 22" (25 x 55 cm). From these pieces cut 11 strips in assorted colors, 3" x 22" (8 x 55 cm). Cut six strips of background fabric, 3" x 44" (8 x 110 cm) then cut these in half at the fold, making 12 strips 3" x 22" (8 x 55 cm).

Sew one strip of background to each of the 11 assorted strips and press the seams to the dark side of the fabric.

Counter-cut each of the assembled strips into six 3" (8 cm) wide pieces.

Match up the 2-patches in a pleasing arrangement. Lay one on top of the other, right sides together, butting the opposing seams, and sew (see page 31). Make 32 of these 4-patches.

Measure an assortment of the 4-patches and calculate the average size (it should be 5½", 14.5 cm). Cut 31 background squares this size by cutting strips and counter-cutting as above. Lay out these squares alternately with the 4-patch blocks in a 9 x 7 format in the desired arrangement. Number the squares and blocks with small sticky labels placed in the center of each.

Sew the squares and blocks together in rows, carefully following the numbered layout. Press the seams toward the background squares (don't iron the sticky labels).

Pin, then sew the rows together in pairs, sewing the last odd row to the bottom pair, then join the sets of rows. Remove the labels. Press the seam allowances to one side. The quilt top should measure 50" x 39" (132 x 103 cm).

Cut and sew the border strips (see Piecing the Quilt Top, page 29). Calculate the dimensions so the completed quilt top width doesn't exceed the width of the backing fabric. If you want to roll the backing fabric over to the top instead of adding a binding, the back should be at least 1" (2.5 cm) larger on each side than the top. Lay out the backing, batting, and quilt top. Tie the quilt (see page 24 for instructions) and bind it (see page 33 for instructions).

The experience of making these 4-patch quilts provided the children with a good knowledge of all the steps involved in quilt making and the confidence to try more complicated piecing for their next projects.

PROJECTS USING CHILDREN'S DESIGNS
GEOMETRY PROJECTS

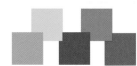

Designing quilt blocks from simple squares, triangles, and rectangles is a creative way to teach some basic concepts of geometry. Teach the children to identify 4-patch, 9-patch, and 16-patch blocks. Show how the patches may be further reduced to smaller squares, triangles, rectangles, diamonds, and even curved pieces. You will be surprised at how quickly the children recognize the patterns and are able to break down any quilt block into the basic units. The paper project is a good way to start and the materials are cheap.

Paper project supplies with sample blocks to demonstrate some patterns.

Geometry Poster: A Paper Project

Geometry Poster
68" x 40"   (170 x 100 cm)

Geometry Poster.

Project participants: 48 children (24 on each poster) ages 6 to 10, The Family Classroom, spring 1997
Minimum recommended age: 6
Level of difficulty: Easy
Sessions with the children: 3
Preparation: 4 hours (cut paper geometric shapes, create and photocopy work sheets, draw block outlines on poster sheet) 2 hours if the children color shapes with crayons instead of sticking paper shapes.

Supplies
* Copies of handout "9-Patch Design Sheet"
* Copies of handout "How many pieces in your design?"
* Copies of handout "9-Patch Layout"
* Pencils, crayons, glue sticks, paper cutting scissors
* Colored paper squares, 2½" (6 cm)
* Colored paper squares, 1¼" (3 cm)
* Colored paper large triangles, 2½" (6 cm) squares cut in half diagonally
* Colored paper small triangles, 2½" (6 cm) squares cut diagonally in both directions
* Colored paper rectangles, 2½" (6 cm) squares cut in half
* Background paper with block and sashing lines marked for the placement of the children's blocks

Preparations

Cut old wallpaper sample books or construction paper into geometric shapes. Using a rotary cutter saves time and is accurate. Estimating the numbers of shapes you will need for the project is difficult. If a child uses small squares for the entire design, 36 are needed to complete the block, but a simple 9-patch will use only nine large squares. We prepared far too many, but some colors were popular and were all used. Extra shapes may be recycled for other projects and geometry exercises. You could start with only large squares, then cut them into small squares, triangles and rectangles as the children need them. Cut a variety of colors and plenty of extras allowing at least 12 large squares per child.

Tape large pieces of colored paper together for the background (butcher paper works well). Mark a grid on which to attach the blocks. This may be set squarely, on the point, with or without sashing strips. The sashing strips separate the blocks and make it easier for the children to identify and point out their own work. You may cut out sashing strips to stick down or leave them blank (the color of the background paper). For possible layouts, see Piecing the Quilt Top, page 29. If you would like the blocks to be placed adjacent, there is no need to draw lines for sashing strips. You may be surprised by the new secondary patterns that emerge between two touching blocks, but it will be more difficult for the children to distinguish their own blocks.

Preparing the Three Handouts

1. 9-Patch Design Sheet (see photo on page 113)
2. How Many Pieces in Your Design?
3. 9-Patch Layout (see photos on pages 113-115)

1. 9-Patch Design Sheet
Draw six blank 9-patches for the children to create their design. At the top of the sheet draw five squares showing how the squares in the design can be divided: large square with no division, two large triangles, two rectangles, four small triangles and four small squares. Below this you can draw some examples (optional) to show the types of possible patterns.

2. How Many Pieces in Your Design?
The design components are itemized so that the children can record how many of each shape they need. Draw the relevant shape to the left of the line item using the same representation from the top of the design sheet:
Large squares
Large triangles
Rectangles
Small Squares
Small Triangles
Total Number of Pieces

3. 9-Patch Layout
Draw the 9-patch grid to scale using 2½" (6cm) squares so that it measures 7½" x 7½" (18 x 18 cm). Include the five squares showing the possible divisions at the top of the sheet.

Working With the Children
Session I: Draw and color the six 9-patches on the "9-Patch Design Sheet" handout. Choose the favorite design and complete the "How Many Pieces in Your Design?" handout.
Session II: Select the colored shapes and stick them on the "9-Patch Layout" handout.
Session III: Arrange the blocks on the paper background and glue them down.

The children use the "9-Patch Design Sheet" to design their own blocks. Show them how the square units may be subdivided into triangles, rectangles, and small squares. Combinations of rectangles and squares, and large and small triangles can also be drawn.

The children should use pencil to subdivide the squares on the grids, then color their patterns.

Next ask them to choose their favorite pattern to make a full-sized block, 7½" (18 cm) square for the poster. They should use the "How Many Pieces in Your Design?" handout to record the numbers of squares, triangles, and rectangles required for the block, then select the correct number of each shape in the desired colors, from boxes of pre-cut colored shapes.

Using the favorite pattern as a guide, glue the colored paper shapes in the appropriate positions on the "9-Patch Layout" handout. When the glue is dry, cut out the block ready for placing on the big colored background paper. The children will enjoy arranging the blocks on the grid. Make sure all the blocks and paper shapes are glued securely so they don't fall off. Laminating the quilt mural will increase the durability and reduce fading. The finished product is sure to brighten up a classroom wall.

Gluing shapes on the 9-patch layout.

A completed paper block.

Geometry Quilt

Project participants: 48 children ages 6 to 10, The Family Classroom, spring 1997
Minimum recommended age: 6
Level of difficulty: Easy
Sessions with the children: 2
Preparation: 16 hours - 8 hours to piece 256 squares - enough for 16 blocks @ 12", 32 cm (get help!), 8 hours to piece blocks before Session II.

Supplies
(see page 25 to estimate fabric quantities)
* Unbleached muslin for 128 squares, 4" (10.5 cm)
* Variety of brightly colored fabrics for 128 squares, 4" (10.5 cm)
* Fabric for frames around blocks, 1½" wide (4 cm)
* Fabric for intersections, 3" square (8 cm)
* Fabric for sashing strips, 3" wide (8 cm)
* Fabric for binding and backing
* 16 squares of paper for pinning out the children's block arrangements, approx. 15" (36 cm)
* Batting

Patchwork Geometry
69" x 69"   (173 x 173 cm)

Organize the children into small groups to design a 16-patch block from 16 fabric squares. The squares are made from two half-square triangles, one of muslin and the other of a bright contrasting color. After the blocks have been pieced, the children may arrange the layout for the quilt.

Preparation

Cut 128 muslin and 128 contrasting squares. Draw a diagonal pencil line in one direction on the back of the muslin squares. Place a muslin and colored square right sides together and machine stitch two seams, each one ¼" (0.75 cm) away from the pencil line.

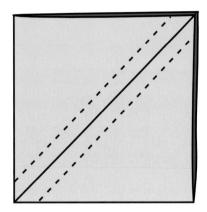

Place a dark and light square right sides together and machine stitch ¼" (0.75 cm) on either side of the diagonal pencil line on the pale squares.

Cut along the pencil line. You will have two pieced squares. Open the squares and press the seams toward the dark fabric.

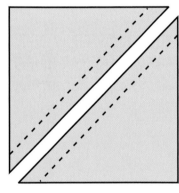

Cut along the pencil line. Open the squares and press the seams toward the dark fabric.

If one person prepares all the squares for the project and is consistent with the seam allowance, all the squares should be the same size. If you have a variety of sizes, trim them all to 3½" (9.5 cm). It is worthwhile doing this because when you piece the blocks, the squares will go together easily without the points of triangles being blunted or the blocks becoming misshapen.

Working With the Children

Children have fun designing the 16 blocks for the quilt and are most creative in the patterns they generate. In Session I divide the children into small groups (divide the number of children by the number of blocks you want to make). Let them play with the 16 squares, turning them and trying out different 4 x 4 arrangements. When I gave our children directions, I demonstrated on a flannel board with a spare package of squares the formation of pinwheels, flying geese, zigzags, and a variety of patterns. I deliberately took my patterns apart before the children started arranging their squares to prevent them from copying. I encouraged them to experiment with several patterns before making their final decision. Some children liked symmetrical regular patterns, and others created irregular designs. Once the group had agreed on their block layout, they pinned the squares to a piece of paper and labeled the top.

Pinning squares to paper.

Before Session II, machine piece the squares together, and use sticky labels or safety pins to mark the top of the blocks. This is time-consuming, so get help!

Back in the classroom for Session II, spread a large bed sheet on the floor on which to arrange the blocks (a dark color looks good - I used purple). A group of 20 to 25 children can sit around the perimeter of the sheet. Some can hardly contain their excitement, but they must sit still! Lay the blocks out at random and allow the children to take turns at switching the positions of two blocks. Make sure the blocks stay the right way up by observing the position of the labeled top edge. Our children were quite particular about this. When a girl commented that she liked the arrangement and didn't want to make any further changes, we had a vote, and the majority agreed with her.

On our quilt, a meandering quilting stitch covered the blocks and the sashing strips were quilted in the ditch.

To elaborate on this project, you could have the children hand stitch the squares. Give each child a package of eight half-square triangles, four darks and four lights, to make four squares. Prepare the triangles using template J, Appendix 6. The preparation time is about the same, but the children will need three additional sessions for sewing. Machine piece the squares into blocks using the pencil seam lines as a guide.

Trying different block arrangements.

Glossary

4-patch block: Block divided into four equal parts (2 x 2).

9-patch block: Block divided into nine equal parts (3 x 3).

16-patch block: Block divided into 16 equal parts (4 x 4).

Adults: Grown-ups who are children at heart!

Album quilt: Quilt in which each block is signed by friends in ink or embroidery.

Appliqué: Process of sewing small pieces of fabric to a larger background piece of fabric.

Assembly line piecing: Machine piecing several fabruc units together one after another without lifting the presser foot or cutting threads between units.

Backstitch: Short stitch used to begin, end, and strengthen the running stitch in hand piecing.

Bargello: Originally a needlepoint term describing certain flowing undulating patterns. Strip piecing techniques in bargello quilting reproduce and elaborate on these types of patterns.

Basting: Process of joining the layers of a quilt together to secure them for quilting. Long running stitches sewn by hand, safety pins, or plastic tacks may be used.

Batt: A piece of batting for a quilt.

Batting (also known as wadding): Fiber used as filling between the quilt top and the quilt backing to provide warmth. It may be cotton, polyester, cotton-polyester blend, wool, or silk.

Betweens: Short, firm needles for quilting. The higher the number, the smaller the needle.

Bias: Diagonal grain in relation to the lengthwise and crosswise grains of a woven fabric.

Binding: Narrow strip of fabric used to cover the raw edges and batting of a quilt. Also, the technique of finishing the edges of the quilt.

Block: Design unit of a quilt top. It may be made of patchwork, appliqué, or a combination, and is often square.

Border: Strip of fabric, which may be pieced, framing the outer edges of a quilt top.

Crazy patchwork: Irregular-shaped pieces stitched to a foundation.

Crazy quilt: Quilt made from crazy patchwork. In Victorian times rich velvets, silks, and other fabrics were used, and often embroidered with elaborate designs. These so-called Victorian "crazy quilts" were not usually quilted and regular shapes such as hexagons and diamonds were frequently used rather than the crazy patchwork.

Cross grain: Woven threads of a fabric that are perpendicular to the selvages.

Cutting mat: Special mat used for rotary cutting to protect the surface beneath the fabric and preserve the sharpness of the blade on the cutter.

Embroidery: Process of sewing decorative stitches.

English piecing: hand piecing technique in which fabric shapes are basted over paper templates and stitched together along their edges.

Fat quarter: 18" x 22" (50 x 56 cm) piece of fabric (quarter of a yard/meter).

Finished size: Measurements of a completed piece, block, or quilt top without the seam allowances.

Foundation piecing: Piecing of fabric patches onto a fabric or paper foundation.

Freezer paper: Butcher paper waxed on one side. Used for stabilizing the fabric during drawing or writing, and in the resist stencil printing technique.

Friendship quilt: Quilt made or signed by friends, or made from scraps provided by friends.

Fusible appliqué: Appliqué using fusible webbing to bond the pieces to the background.

Half-square triangle: Triangle made by cutting a square diagonally in half.

Hawaiian appliqué: Traditional Hawaiian technique in which a large appliqué design is made by folding the fabric and cutting it to create a symmetrical design. This design often fills the whole quilt and is attached to the background by needle-turned hand appliqué.

Lengthwise grain: Woven fabric threads that run parallel to the selvages.

Medallion quilt: Pieced or appliquéd quilt with a large central motif or design surrounded by borders.

On point: Block setting in which the block is placed with its sides at 45° to the edge of the quilt.

Patch: Individual fabric shape to be used in patchwork.

Patchwork: Fabric made up of small pieces of fabric sewn together.

Piecing: Joining of patchwork pieces by hand or machine stitching.

Quilt: Two layers of fabric (the top and the backing), separated by a layer of batting and joined together with quilting stitches.

Quilting: Act of securing the three layers of the quilt together with quilting stitches. Also, the act of making a quilt.

Quilting bee: Social gathering for the purpose of quilting, traditionally at a large quilting frame.

Quilting frame: Large freestanding frame used for holding the layers of the quilt together for quilting.

Quilting hoop: Tool used to hold a small portion of the quilt taut for quilting.

Quilting stitches: Small stitches that hold the three layers of the quilt together and may also form decorative patterns.

Quilting thread: Special type of thread used for hand quilting, usually stronger than regular sewing thread.

Quilt top: Completed patchwork, appliqué, or wholecloth top of the quilt that is ready to be joined to the batting and backing to make the quilt.

Right side: Front or top side of the fabric.

Rotary cutter: Fabric cutting tool with a circular blade that may be used to cut through several layers of fabric at once.

Ruching: Fabric strip that has been tucked and gathered before being appliquéd to the background fabric.

Running stitch: Short even stitch used for hand piecing.

Sampler quilt: Quilt in which all the blocks are of differing patterns.

Sashing: Strip of fabric pieced between two blocks to separate them.

Seam allowance: Margin of fabric between the seam and the raw edge (standard is ¼", 0.75 cm).

Selvage: Lengthwise finished edge on each side of the fabric.

Snippets: Small pieces of fabric backed with fusible webbing, used in creating fusible appliqué designs.

Stipple quilting: Close background quilting (less than ½", 1.5 cm apart) used to create a surface texture and raise the area it surrounds.

Straight grain: Woven threads of the fabric running parallel and perpendicular to the selvage, i.e. the cross grain and the lengthwise grain.

Strip piecing: Technique in which strips of fabric are cut and joined lengthwise, then cut across the seam lines to form segments. The segments are joined to create units or blocks for the quilt top.

Templates: Shapes made of sturdy material used to trace designs on fabric. They can be used for marking fabric for piecing or for marking quilting lines.

Tied quilt: Quilt in which ties are used to hold the three layers of the quilt together. Technically, these are comforters and not quilts since they have no quilting stitches.

Trapunto: Technique in which the quilt surface is raised by stuffing from behind.

Unfinished size: Size of a strip or fabric piece before it is joined to other pieces of fabric. Also used for blocks and completed quilt tops. The unfinished size includes the seam allowance.

Whole-cloth quilt: Quilt in which the top consists of one large piece of fabric with no decorative patchwork or appliqué.

Wrong side: Back or underside of the fabric.

Project Participants

Most of the projects took place in 1994 and 1997 at Wilkes Elementary School, Blakely Elementary School, and The Alternative Elementary School. These three public schools are in the Bainbridge Island School District, Washington.

The 1997 projects at Blakely Elementary School and The Family Classroom (The Alternative School) were documented photographically as they progressed. Camp Fire Girls, Girl Scouts, and children with four block sampler quilts were also photographed. For these projects all the children's names are listed. For other projects in which a quilt is featured, but the children were not photographed, the children's names are not listed. All the quilts were quilted by machine unless otherwise specified.

Blakely Elementary School, Bainbridge Island, Spring 1997

All the projects were designed and coordinated by Maggie Ball and M.J. Linford. Lisa Jowise organized the parent volunteers who gave over 100 hours of help. Principal Ric Jones granted permission and made the facilities available, and Judy Carlbom, school secretary, provided administrative and moral support.

Forest Fantasy: Sonnie Anderson, Lance Armstrong, Jessica Ballou, Keziah Beall, Chelsea Bell, Michael Buetow, Spencer Byl, Miles Drake, Nicholas Herbst, Chad Kakela, Elizabeth Klous, Thomas Kribble, Electra Magnuson, Shelby Mann, Jerry McKee, Kristie Smith, Riley Smith, Dylan Tucker-Gangnes, Sophie Wenzlau, Sarah Wettleson, and Evan Wright. Pieced by Lisa Jowise, quilted by Vi Griffiths. Owned by Maggie Ball.

Tree of Life: Travis D'Allesandro, Bryan Dever, Lauren Ginder, Tessa Griffin, Kyle Grosten, Nicholas Janetos, Erin Kratzer, Jocelyn Maher, Micah Omaits, Diana Poncé, Daniel Quinn, Emily Schuetz, Elizabeth Shrosbee, Cody Somers, Kyle Thomas, Morgan Wainio, Claire Williamson, Sarah Willis, Azia Wisdom, Curtis Wright, and Kristina Zimmers. Pieced by Maggie Ball, quilted by Sharon Carlson. Owned by Blakely Elementary School.

Woodland Walk: John Baggett, Emily Bell, Melissa Cini, Matt Dueñas, Devin Freimark, Willy Greene, Johanna Holliday, Anna Houk, Katherine Hutcheson, Sean Lappi, Peter Leslie, Jessie McMillan, Jacquelyn Oakland, Anna Pollock, Chyna Riedel, Wesley Saunders, Lexi Schmidt, Brandon Scott, Joel Turkheimer, Paul Varner, Ned Whalen. Pieced by Maggie Ball, quilted by Becky Hanson. Owned by Blakely Elementary School.

Friendship Tree: Mariah Ahern, Vanessa Brewis-Condon, Katherine Cash, Adrian Charvet, Bret Crane, Taylor Eliason, Tyler Ferrell, Mac Griffiths, Gus Julian, Winston McBride, Alexander Medina, Katie Paeth, Maggie Pool, Jonathan Potter, Sarah Ramadan, Mathew Ritualo, Matthew Saboda, Martha Slichter, Ben Tift, and Stephanie Whitmore. Pieced by Lisa Jowise and quilted by Dana Taylor. Owned by Blakely Elementary School.

Winter Star: Kyla Barr, Phillip Benjamin, Ryan Bohannon, Jason Bohnert, Corey Cross, Robert Frease, Dalton Gent, Erin Gulbranson, Marley Horne, Jessica Johnson, Jennifer Jurca, Paxton Kruse, Samuel Kuhn, Mara Lang, Laura Lyons, Kelsey Middleton, Naty Moncada, Josephine Nickum, Jonathan Nyhus, Margaret Olsen, Lilly Parsons, Emily Peters, Liberty Rothbaum, Miranda Saunders, and Adam Tyner. Pieced by Maggie Ball and quilted by Laurie Vilbrandt. Owned by Blakely Elementary School.

Frosty Window: Alexander Beard, Connor Cioc, Patrick Dight, Carmen Duran, Carol Earnest, Andrew Emau, Lucie Gendreau, Stuart Hanberg, Cory Jellicoe, Kristen Jones, Maxwell Jowise, Kevin Keller, Olivia Lee,

Alison Loechl, Claire Luke, Tabitha Mabrey, Jacquie Menalia, James Neill, Marijke Smith, Jamie Slonaker, Robert Stevenson, Kayla Swerin, Emma White, and Lindsay White. Pieced by Lisa Jowise and quilted by Larkin Van Horn. Owned by Blakely Elementary School.

Winter Wonderland: Melissa Ahneman, Megan Burris, Alexander Carter, Shannon Clagett, Jesse Colkitt, Rye Cook-Biggert, Daniel Cox, Kerry Hillier, Kris Hillis, Samuel Hobbs, Jessie McGrath, Catie Mirkovich, Helen Moga, Andrew Powers, Nash Reijnen, Kathleen Shurtleff, Naomi Smith, Alexander Steele, Kristy Taylor, Emily Thomas, Patrick Wauters, Hannah Weisser, Chelsea Whealdon, and Erin Wilmot. Pieced by Maggie Ball and quilted by Tammy Stoll. Owned by Maggie Ball.

Crazy Heart: David Arnold, Austin Atendido, Courtney Atkinson, Kaitlin Bailey, Kristine Bell, Amelia Burns, Andrew Byl, Tyler Caughie, Lizzie Dameron, Clayton Habecker, Jurell Houston, Brendan Johnson, Skyler Johnston, Tobin Kerns, Rebecca Lantz, Shawna Leader, Jacquelyn McCormick, Theordore Miller, Katie O'Mara, G.R. Rees, Shelby Semon, John Shrosbree, Timothy Spenser, and Kayley Turkheimer. Pieced and quilted by Maggie Ball, and tied by the children. Owned by Blakely Elementary School.

Hearts Together: Rebecca Armitage, Dane Armstrong, Courtney Bell, Sean Brachvogel, Brittany Bundrant, Austin Charvet, Megan Clark, Lara Dorsett, Jacqueline Fentress, Rachel Frease, Jacob Freimark, Gesele Gellé, Brian Glaser, Diego Gonzalez-Medina, Evan Hodos, Lauren Jay, Laura Kirkwood, Dillon Maslach, Adrian Mason, Emily Robinson, Callie Tift, Matthew Vasicek, Kathryn Vreedenburgh, and Adam Wade. Pieced by Joanne Bennett and quilted by Maggie Ball. Owned by Maggie Ball.

Holiday Hearts: Katie Allen, Elizabeth Annis, Claire Buetow, Nicole Caccioppo, Greg Carlson, Evan Chamberlain, Callan Cobb, Megan Elslip, Sean Forsyth, Brenden Gent, Cody Gramstad, Joe Henderson, Veronica Holmes, William Hutcheson, Alex Jungnitz, Anna Lyons, Morgan Oakland, Jeffrey Pritchard, Zachary Schmidt, Hazel Scott, Rachel Stern, Lauren Trageser, Seth Watson, Stephanie Whalen, and Cole Zwicker. Pieced by Maggie Ball and quilted by Janine Hunt. Owned by Blakely Elementary School.

Four Patch Hearts: Erika Bergman, David McIntyre, Brandi Nelson, and Alexa Lee Seidl. Pieced and quilted by Maggie Ball. Owned by Blakely Elementary School.

Octopus's Garden: Karlyn Adams, Veronica Caroll, Patrick Colegrove, Claire Colegrove, Sam Cooley, Becky Dixon-Gordon, Mariah Edwards, Tiffany Eliason, Kali Ann Ferrell, Christopher Glidden, Tyler Hannon, Henry Hobbs, Thomas Houston, Benjamin James, Roarke Kamber, Emily Kight, Lena McClelland, Shannon McGreal, Michelle Miller, Jocelyn Moody, Timothy Patmont, Leah Preble, Joe Reynolds, Read Slichter, Jacqueline Smith, Adam Stanger, and their homeroom teacher, Maureen Pitinga-Wilson. Pieced by Maggie Ball and M.J. Linford, and quilted by Becky Hanson. Owned by Blakely Elementary School.

Under the Sea: Maureen Pitinga-Wilson's class as listed above. Pieced by Maggie Ball and M.J. Linford and quilted by Maggie Ball. Owned by Maggie Ball.

Super Silly Animals: Peter Bech, Laura Browne, Tyler Bural, Samuel Cameron, Theodora Carson, Ryan Carson, Dana Cuykendall, Nicholas Duran, Scott Flodin, Aaron Frease, Meghan Gladstein, Adriana Gonzalez-Medina, Jonathan Holmes, Johnny James, Katie Kratzer, Lia Layton, Lee Maloney, Kyle McFarlane, Logan Mohr, Harte Onewein, Maggie Pettit, Catherine Powers, Allana Pritchard, Christopher Rauch, Jack Sassenfeld, William Silva, Stephanie Springer and Anthony Wheaton. Pieced by Lisa Jowise and quilted by O'Della Kelly. Owned by Maggie Ball.

Absolutely Awesome Animals: Trent Adams, Taylor Anderson, Grace Armstrong, Christopher Cioc, Mary Doyle, Laura Earnest, Rebecca Ferrell, Crystal Glaser, Nathan Gottlieb, Derek Houston, Nicole Ing, Veronica Ivey, Michaela Jellicoe, Peter Jowise, Bill Kirkwood, Matthew Koehler, Kara

Mann, Michael McCreery, Lauren Nease, Aaron Olanie, Amy Paeth, Dylan Preble, Kassie Soni, Jennifer Talbert, Matthew Wauters, Carl Webster, Morgan Weisser, and Sofia Willis. Pieced by Janine Hunt and quilted by Lillie Fontaine. Owned by Blakely Elementary School.

Happy Hilarious Animals: Ashley Anderson, Mallory Betz, Colleen Burke, Mehgan Colkitt, Ian Faulk, Sean Gallagher, Tiana Gallagher, Nathan Gidney, Bradford Girtz, Eddie Henderson, Nicole Henshaw, Randy Herzog, Mali Hillis, Nate Houk, Tristan Jungnitz, Mathias Klous III, Morgan Lee, Christoper Lyons, Monica Meell, Cally Owens, Genevieve Pritchard, Angelo Ritualo, Nick Schuetz, Crecia Scovill, Cody Semon, Allison Sterrett, Skylar Wilkins, Lacey Wilmot and David Yesland. Pieced by Pat Reynolds and quilted by Glynis Burns. Owned by Blakely Elementary School.

Heart-felt Thanks: All of the Blakely children listed above. Quilt designed, coordinated and pieced by M.J. Linford and Lisa Jowise, and quilted by Dana Taylor. Owned by Maggie Ball.

The Family Classroom, Bainbridge Island Alternative School, Spring 1997

The 48 children ages 6 to 10 years, participated in making five quilts. All the children contributed towards the geometry quilt. For the other four quilts the children were divided into two groups of 24, each group making two quilts. Maggie Ball coordinated all the projects in collaboration with the teachers, Peggy Koivu, and Casey Jeffers. Judy McCrudden and Kathy Bergum organized the parent volunteers, and Bruce Colley, Principal, granted permission and made the facilities available.

Children participants: Max Aussendorf, Lacey Blankenship, Page Bonifaci, Chloe Carl, Nina Kunzi-Clark, Lauren Cuykendall, Justin Donais, David Elliot, Rosie Fisher-Sergent, Ramona Freeborn, Colin Gremse, Valerie Halm, Kirsten Hartz, Erica Hemmen, Zena Hemmen, Allison Hepp, Spencer Hepp, Zach Ingrasci, Miles Johnson, John Leatherman, Corbin Lester, Katarina Lunde, John Major, Sidney Mattocks, Jamie Maurer, Pepper Dekker-McCormick, Christina McCrudden, Derry McDonald, Alyssa Merenbach, Ian Powell, Thea Reinhert, Billy Russell, Samuel Sellers, Alec Sloane, Emile Stettler, Natalie Stewart, Clarie Tilton, Melanie Tilton, Delsa Toglia, Francis Toglia, John David Toren, Aaron Van Dyke, Libbey Van Dyke, Gabe Vittum, Evan Walker, Jeremy Watson, Kalila Zunes-Wolfe, and Shanti Zunes-Wolfe.

Patchwork Geometry: 48 children as listed above. Pieced by Mavis Tullis, Wanda Rains and Maggie Ball, and quilted by Tammy Stoll. Owned by Maggie Ball.

Dragon Heart: 24 of the children listed above hand pieced the 4-patch blocks and embroidered the hearts. Maggie Ball assembled the blocks, and the quilting was by Laurie Vilbrandt. Owned by The Family Classroom.

Brave Heart: 24 of the children listed above hand pieced the 4-patches and embroidered the hearts. Maggie Ball assembled the blocks. The quilt was machine quilted by Maggie Ball, and hand quilted and tied by the children. Owned by Maggie Ball.

Historical Bainbridge Island: 24 of the children listed above illustrated the blocks. The quilt was pieced by Maggie Ball and quilted by Maria Groat. Owned by Maggie Ball.

Bainbridge Island Past and Present: 24 of the children listed above illustrated the blocks. The quilt was pieced by Maggie Ball and quilted by Mary Rucker. Owned by The Family Classroom.

Wilkes Elementary School, Bainbridge Island, Spring 1994

The eight quilts featured in this book are a selection from a school-wide project in which every class made a quilt and over 500 children participated. 21 quilts were made and auctioned at a PTO fund-raiser. Principal Kristina Mayer, allowed us to embark on this ambitious project and made the facilities available. Liz Potter, School Secretary, provided administrative and moral support, and the teachers cooperated enthusiastically. The Librarian, Patti Schlosser, was particularly supportive. All the projects were designed and coordinated by Wendy Simon and Maggie Ball in collaboration with the teachers. Too many volunteers to name (over 60), helped with the quilts and the organization of the auction. Those particularly valuable in assisting Wendy and Maggie with the quilts featured in this book were: Carol Hasko, Mary Kay Johncock, Margaret Mathisson, Karla Nelson, and Maja Stone.

Helping Hands Banner: 24 children and teacher, Kathy Dunn. Pieced and quilted by Wendy Simon. Owned by Kathy Dunn.

All About Me: 20 children and teacher, Charlene White. Pieced by Maggie Ball and quilted by Lillie Fontaine. Owned by Julie Houck.

Catch This: 22 children and teacher, Mary Lou Upton. Pieced by Wendy Simon and quilted by Kathy Concannon. Owned by Barbara Carver.

Scenes of a Working Harbor: 26 children and teacher, Alice Mendoza. Pieced and quilted by Wendy Simon. Owned by Kris Hotchkiss.

Save the Rain Forest: 25 children and teacher, Susan Dew. Pieced by Maggie Ball and quilted by Kathy Concannon. Owned by Donna Kuchin.

Endangered Species: 27 children and teacher, Anne Lertora. Pieced by Maggie Ball and hand quilted by the children. Owned by Donna Kuchin.

A History of Bainbridge Island: 26 children and teacher, Karin Torgerson. Hand appliquéd by the children, pieced by Maggie Ball and quilted by Wendy Simon. Owned by Bainbridge Island Public Library.

Pioneer Patchwork: 26 children and teacher, Mary Madison. Blocks hand sewn by the children, pieced and quilted by Wendy Simon. Owned by Jim Gunderson.

Wilkes Elementary School, Bainbridge Island, Spring 1997

Self Portrait Quilt: 24 children. Project designed and coordinated by Judy Weiland and the teacher, Kathy Dunn. The quilt was hand quilted by Leslie Lieman, Donna McDonald, and Judy Weiland. Owned by Donna McDonald.

The Island School, Bainbridge Island, Spring 1997

Medieval Memories: All grade levels from kindergarten to fourth (90 children). The project was designed and coordinated by Cindy Brickley with the help of parent volunteers, Sue Lukins, Laura O'Mara, Pam Gidari, and Celia Clark. The quilting was by Wendy Simon. Owned by Kate Webster.

St. Barnabas Episcopal Church, Bainbridge Island, 1994-95

Retreat Quilt: Project designed and coordinated by Maggie Ball. 36 parishioners illustrated blocks for the quilt during a family retreat at Port Townsend, Washington. Hand quilted by these and other parishioners. Owned by St. Barnabas Episcopal Church.

Bainbridge Island High School, Spring 1997

Exploring Childhood Preschool Quilt: 12 preschool and 4 high school students participated. The project was designed and coordinated by high school freshman, Hazel Ball, with the permission of the Exploring Childhood instructor, Susan Nielsen, and preschool teacher Lori Kelly. Pieced and quilted by Maggie Ball. Owned by Hazel Ball.

Hyla Middle School, Bainbridge Island, Spring 1999

Fantasy Coral Reef: 24 children. The project was designed and coordinated by Maggie Ball and art teacher, Laura Jones. The quilt was pieced by Maggie Ball, and quilted by Wanda Rains and Maggie Ball. Owned by Pam McNulty.

Groups working on Individual Projects
Girl Scouts, Bainbridge Island

4-Patch Quilts, 1996: Kristi Sutton coordinated, taught and encouraged this group of 10 eighth, ninth and tenth grade girls to make their own 4-patch quilts. Project designed by Margaret Mathisson and Wendy Simon. Emily Wiedenhoeft, Paula Sutton, and Sarah Weigle were photographed.

Camp Fire Group, Bainbridge Island

Patchwork pillows, 1996 and 1997: Kay Larson coordinated the group and Maggie Ball led the patchwork pillow project. Hazel Ball, Sarah Collier, Heather Fuller, Sarah Hedderly-Smith, Zoe Reeves and Sushi Speidel made pillows.

Wilkes Elementary School Extra-curricular Program, 1995

Four Block Sampler Quilts: Wendy Simon and Maggie Ball taught a four-session class in which 12 children in the third, fourth and fifth grades each made their own small sampler quilt. Children and their quilts featured in this book: Katie Bailey, Emily Hallet, Ashely Hempelmann, Caitlin Kiley, Lindsey Mundt, Katie Norrie, Gretchen Pedersen and Molly Weiland.

Individual and Small Group Projects

Penguins on Parade, Spring 1997: Blocks illustrated by Nigel, Maggie, Hazel and Thomas Ball. Pieced and quilted by Maggie Ball. Owned by Thomas Ball.

Fishes and Best Wishes for M.J., Spring 1997: Fish prints by Hazel Ball and Sushi Speidel. Pieced and quilted by Maggie Ball. Owned by M.J. Linford.

Eric the Fish, Spring 1997: Fish print and painting by Hazel Ball. Pieced and quilted by Maggie Ball. Owned by Hazel Ball.

Water World: Robert (Bobby) Henry, 1996. Quilted by Marilyn Doheny. Owned by Marilyn Dohney

Grassicket and *Menorah*: Breilyn Doheny, 1997. Quilted by Tammy Stoll. Owned by Breilyn Doheny.

Appendix 1
Traditional Block Designs

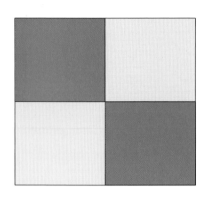

4-Patch: Simple 4-Patch

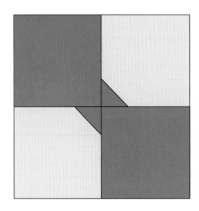

4-Patch: Bowtie or Necktie

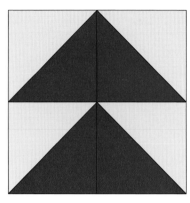

4-Patch: Flying Geese

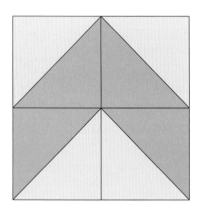

4-Patch: Chevron or Streak of Lightning

4-Patch: Sawtooth

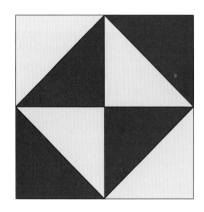

4-Patch: Broken Dishes

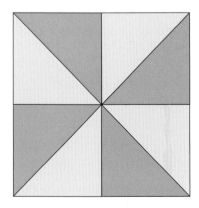

4-Patch: Pinwheel

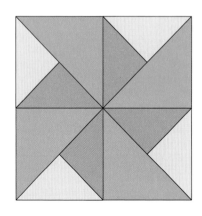

4-Patch: Double Pinwheel or Old Windmill

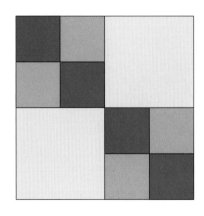

4-Patch: Double 4-Patch

4-Patch: Roman Stripe Zigzag

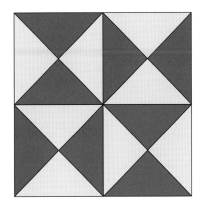

4-Patch: Big Dipper

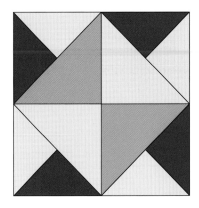

4-Patch: Southern Belle

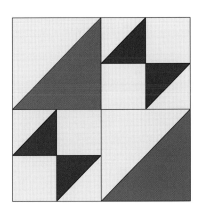

Challenging 4-Patch: Fox and Geese

9-Patch: Simple 9-Patch

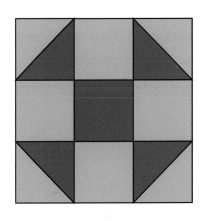

9-Patch: Shoo Fly

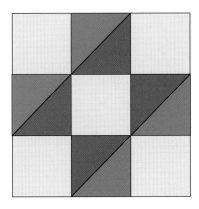

9-Patch: Contrary Wife

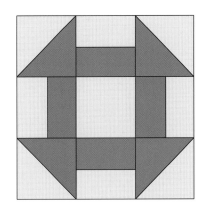

9-Patch: Churn Dash or Monkey Wrench

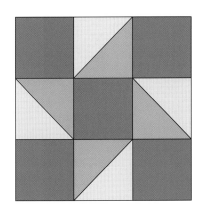

9-Patch: Wings in a Whirl

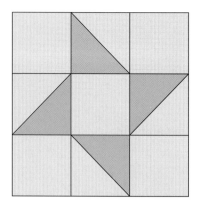

9-Patch: Friendship Star

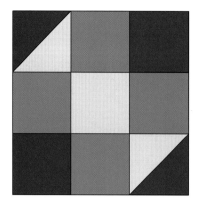

9-Patch: Hourglass

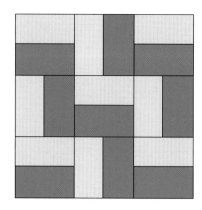

9-Patch: London Stairs

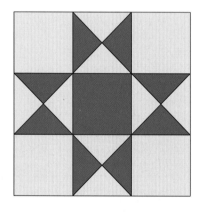

Challenging 9-Patch: Ohio Star

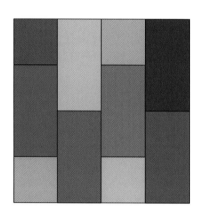

1-Patch: Brick Wall

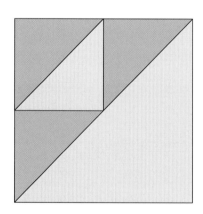

1-Patch: Birds in the Air

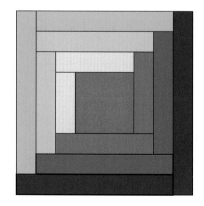

Challenging 1-Patch: Log Cabin

Appliqué: Sunbonnet Sue

Appliqué: Heart

TEMPLATE	TEMPLATE DESCRIPTION (Finished size)	BLOCKS USING TEMPLATE
A	Square - 4½" (12 cm)	Simple 4-patch, Bowtie, Double 4-patch
B	Triangle - ½ of 4½" square (½ of 12 cm square)	Flying Geese, Chevron, Sawtooth, Broken Dishes, Pinwheel, Old Windmill, Southern Belle, Birds in the Air, Fox and Geese
C	Triangle - ¼ of 4½" square (¼ of 12 cm square)	Old Windmill, Big Dipper, Southern Belle
D	Strip - 1½ x 4½" (4 x 12 cm)	Roman Stripe Zig-Zag
E	Square - 4½" (12 cm) with corner cut off	Bowtie
F	Square - 2¼" (6 cm)	Double 4-patch, Brick Wall, Fox and Geese, metric Log Cabin
G	Triangle - ½ of 2¼" (6 cm) square	Bowtie, Fox and Geese
H	Square - 3" (8 cm) For metric Log Cabin use F - 6 cm square	Simple 9-patch, Shoo Fly, Contrary Wife, Churn Dash, Wings in a Whirl, Friendship Star, Hourglass, Ohio Star, Log Cabin
J	Triangle - ½ of 3" (8 cm) square	Shoo Fly, Contrary Wife, Churn Dash, Wings in a Whirl, Friendship Star, Hourglass
K	Triangle - ¼ of 3" (8 cm) square	Ohio Star
L	Strip - 1½" x 3" (4 x 8 cm)	Churn Dash, London Stairs
M	Strip - 2¼" x 4½" (6 x 12 cm)	Brick Wall
N	Triangle - ½ of 9" (24 cm) square See below for drafting instructions	Birds in the Air
Log 1	Strip - 1" x 3" (3 x 6 cm)	Log Cabin
Logs 2 + 3	Strip - 1" x 4" (3 x 9 cm)	Log Cabin
Logs 4 + 5	Strip - 1" x 5" (3 x 12 cm)	Log Cabin
Logs 6 + 7	Strip - 1" x 6" (3 x 15 cm)	Log Cabin
Logs 8 + 9	Strip - 1" x 7" (3 x 18 cm)	Log Cabin
Logs 10 + 11	Strip - 1" x 8" (3 x 21 cm)	Log Cabin
Log 12	Strip - 1" x 9" (3 x 24 cm)	Log Cabin
Heart	Whole heart for 9" (24 cm) block	Heart (appliqué)
S1 - S5	Dress, bonnet, boots, arm, hand	Sunbonnet Sue (appliqué)

Instructions for Drafting Template N

Using graph paper and a sharp pencil, draw a 9" (24 cm) square. Divide the square in two by drawing a diagonal line between two opposite corners. The two triangles formed are Template N for hand sewing. To make a template for machine piecing, add a ¼" (0.75 cm) margin around each edge of one of the triangles. Like the template diagrams provided in Appendix 6, this may easily be traced onto gridded template plastic.

Appendix 3
Block Piecing Instructions
For 4-Patch Blocks

BLOCK PATTERN	TEMPLATES AND SUGGESTED FABRICS	PIECING INSTRUCTIONS
Simple 4-patch	4 x A 2 dark, 2 light	Join squares in pairs. Join the pairs.
Bowtie	2 x A light 2 x E dark 2 x G dark same as E	Join Gs to Es to form squares. Proceed as in 4-patch.
Flying Geese	8 x B 4 dark, 4 light	Join dark and light triangles in pairs to form squares. Proceed as in 4-patch.
Chevron or Streak Lightning	8 x B 4 dark, 4 light	Same as Flying Geese.
Sawtooth	8 x B 4 dark, 4 light	Same as Flying Geese.
Broken Dishes	8 x B 4 dark, 4 light	Same as Flying Geese.
Pinwheel	8 x B 4 dark, 4 light	Same as Flying Geese.
Double Pinwheel or Old Windmill	4 x B medium 8 x C 4 dark, 4 light	Join light and dark small triangles C in pairs to form large triangles. Join these to triangles B to form squares. Proceed as in 4-patch.
Double 4-patch	8 x F 4 dark, 4 light 2 x A light	Join light and dark squares F in pairs. Join these pairs to form large squares. Proceed as in 4-patch.
Roman Stripe Zig-Zag	12 x D 4 dark, 8 light	Join strips together in threes to form squares the same size as A. Proceed as in 4-patch.
Big Dipper	16 x C 8 dark, 8 light	Join light and dark triangles in pairs to form large triangles. Join large triangles in pairs to form squares the same size as A. Proceed as in 4-patch.
Southern Belle	4 x B 2 dark, 2 light 8 x C 4 dark, 4 light	Same as Old Windmill.
Fox and Geese	4 x B 2 dark, 2 light 4 x F 4 light 8 x G 4 dark, 4 light	Join light and dark triangles G in pairs to form squares. Join light and dark triangles B in pairs to form squares. Proceed as in Double 4-patch.

Appendix 4
Block Piecing Instructions
For 9-Patch Blocks

BLOCK PATTERN	TEMPLATES AND SUGGESTED FABRICS	PIECING INSTRUCTIONS
Simple 9-patch	9 x H 5 dark, 4 light or 4 dark, 5 light	Join squares in rows of three. Join rows together.
Shoo Fly	5 x H 1 dark, 4 light 8 x J 4 dark, 4 light	Join light and dark triangles J in pairs to form squares. Proceed as in 9-patch.
Contrary Wife	5 x H light 8 x J 4 dark, 4 light	Same as Shoo Fly.
Churn Dash or Monkey Wrench	1 x H light 8 x J 4 dark, 4 light 8 x L 4 dark, 4 light	Join light and dark Ls in pairs to form squares. Proceed as in Shoo Fly.
Wings in a Whirl	5 x H medium 8 x J 4 dark, 4 light	Same as Shoo Fly.
Friendship Star	5 x H light 8 x J 4 dark, 4 light	Same as Shoo Fly.
Hourglass	7 x H 2 dark, 1 light, 4 medium 4 x J 2 dark, 2 light	Join light and dark triangles J in pairs to form squares. Proceed as in 9-patch.
London Stairs	18 x L 9 dark, 9 light	Join light and dark strips L in pairs to form squares. Proceed as in 9-patch.
Ohio Star	5 x H light 16 x K 8 dark, 8 light	Join light and dark triangles K in pairs to form large triangles. Join large triangles in pairs to form squares. Proceed as in 9-patch.

Block Piecing Instructions
For 1-Patch & Appliqué Blocks

BLOCK PATTERN	TEMPLATES AND SUGGESTED FABRICS	PIECING INSTRUCTIONS
Brick Wall	6 X M variety 4 x F variety	Join bricks together to form four strips. Join strips in pairs. Join pairs of strips.
Birds in the Air	4 x B 3 dark, 1 light 1 x N light or medium (Draft template N)	Join a dark triangle B to a light triangle B. Add the other two dark triangles B to form a large triangle. Join to large triangle N.
Sunbonnet Sue	10" (27 cm) square pale background S1-5 two calico prints and a skin tone	Appliqué Use fusible webbing or lightweight fusible interfacing (see page 19 for instructions).
Heart	10" (27 cm) square background Contrasting fabric for heart Heart template for 9" (24 cm) block	Appliqué - as for Sunbonnet Sue Use the template, or design your own heart and add embellishments.
Log Cabin	1 x H (F for metric Log Cabin) traditionally red or yellow Logs 1-12 - See below.	Logs should be attached to center square in numerical order. See detailed instructions below.

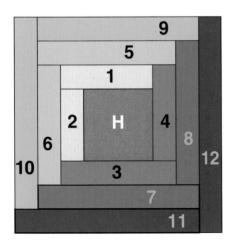

Log Cabin Logs 1, 2, 5, 6, 9, and 10 should be light graduating to medium, with Logs 1 and 2 being the lightest. Logs 3, 4, 7, 8, 11, and 12 should be medium graduating to dark, with Logs 11 and 12 being the darkest. Refer to the diagram below in which the logs are numbered. Start piecing the block from the center. Attach Log 1 to H and finger press the seam to avoid making a tuck when the next log is added. If the piecing is accurate, Log 2 will be an exact fit. Add the logs in numerical order, finger pressing after each one, until the block is complete.

Finished size - 9" square. Size descriptions for metric templates are in Appendix 2.

Dotted inner lines mark the templates for hand piecing.
Solid outer lines mark the templates for machine piecing.
Arrows indicate straight grain of fabric.

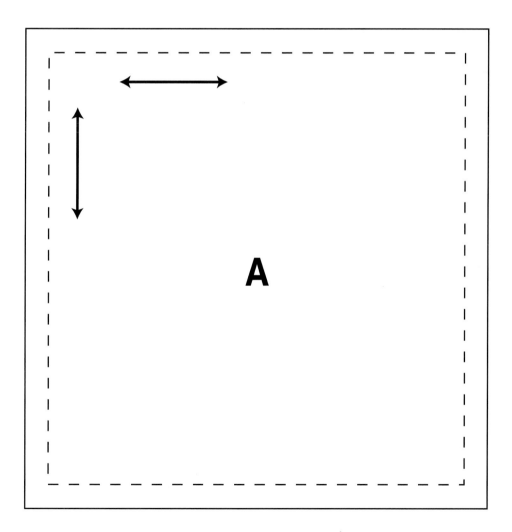

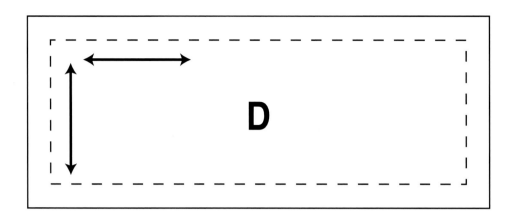

D

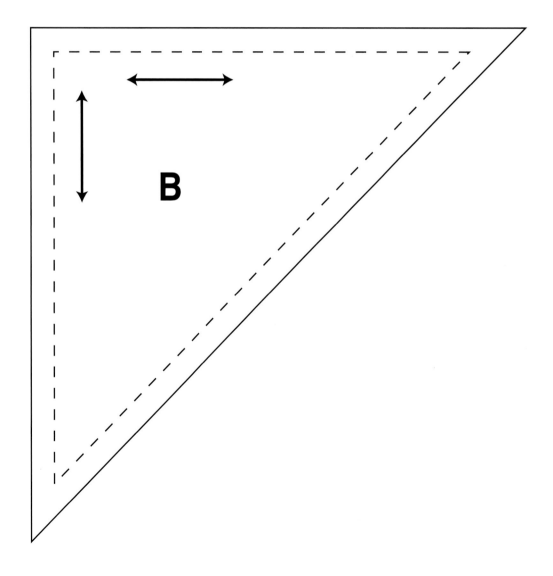

B

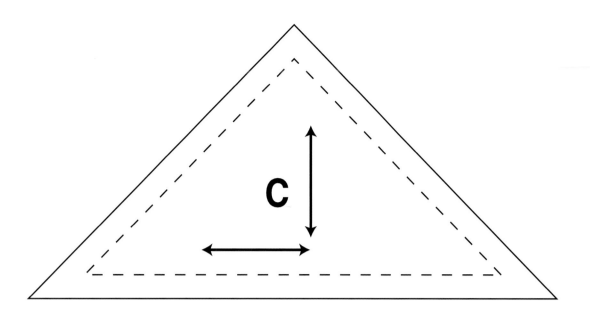

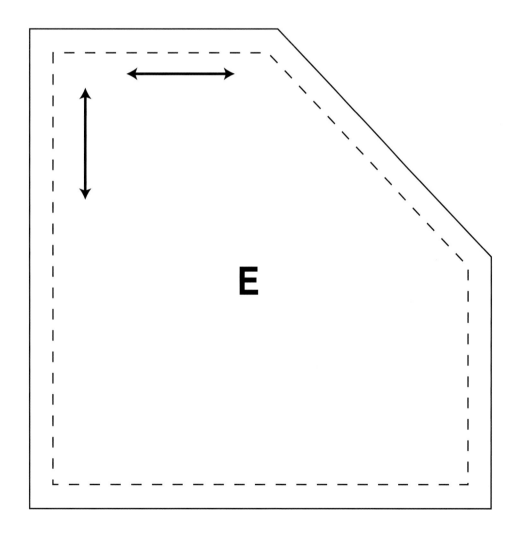

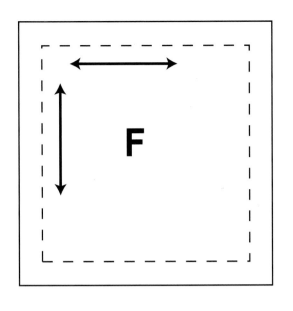

F

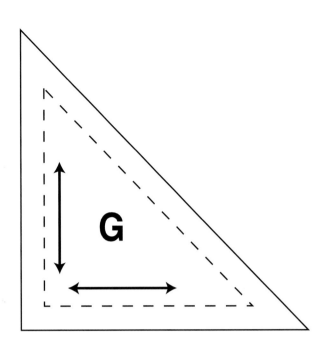

G

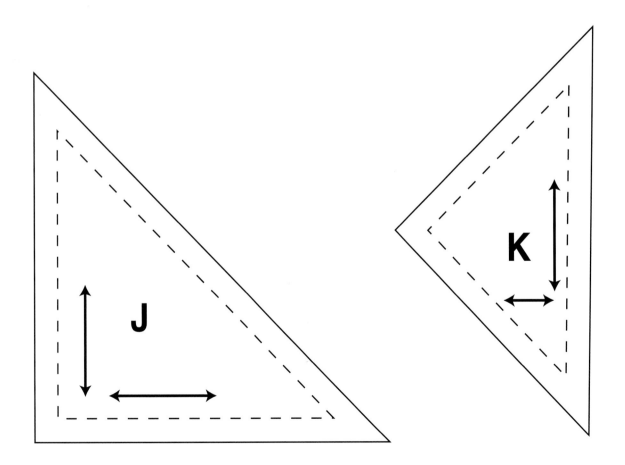

J

K

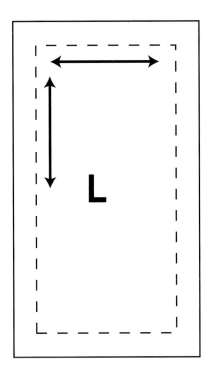

L

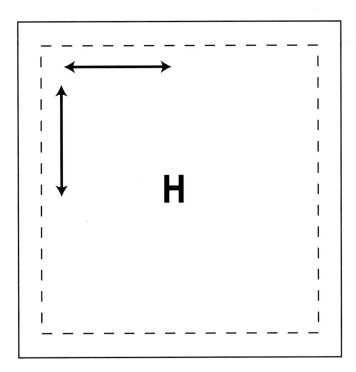

H

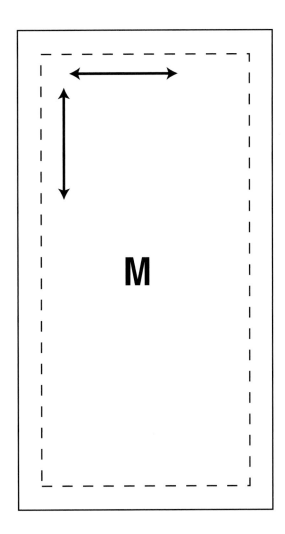

M

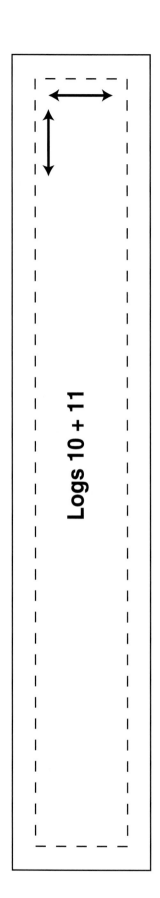

Logs 10 + 11

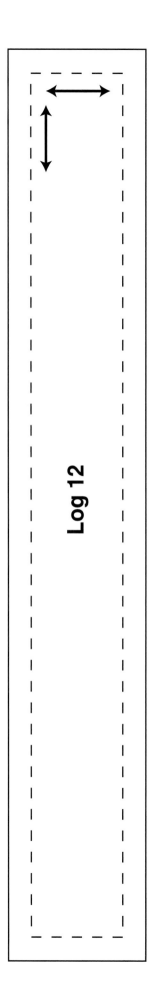

Log 12

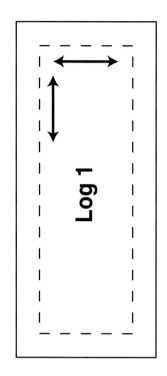

Log 1

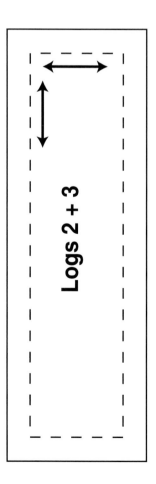

Logs 2 + 3

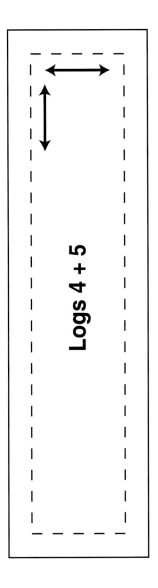

Logs 4 + 5

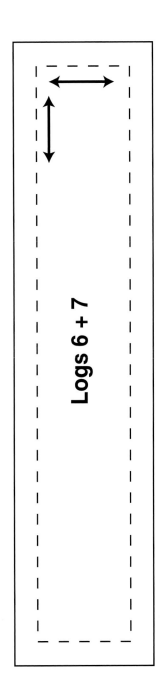

Logs 6 + 7

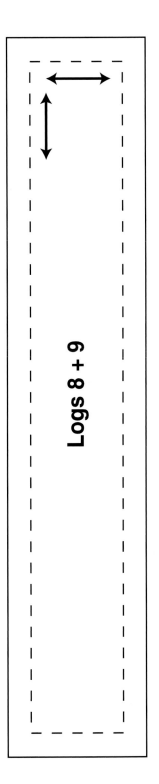

Logs 8 + 9

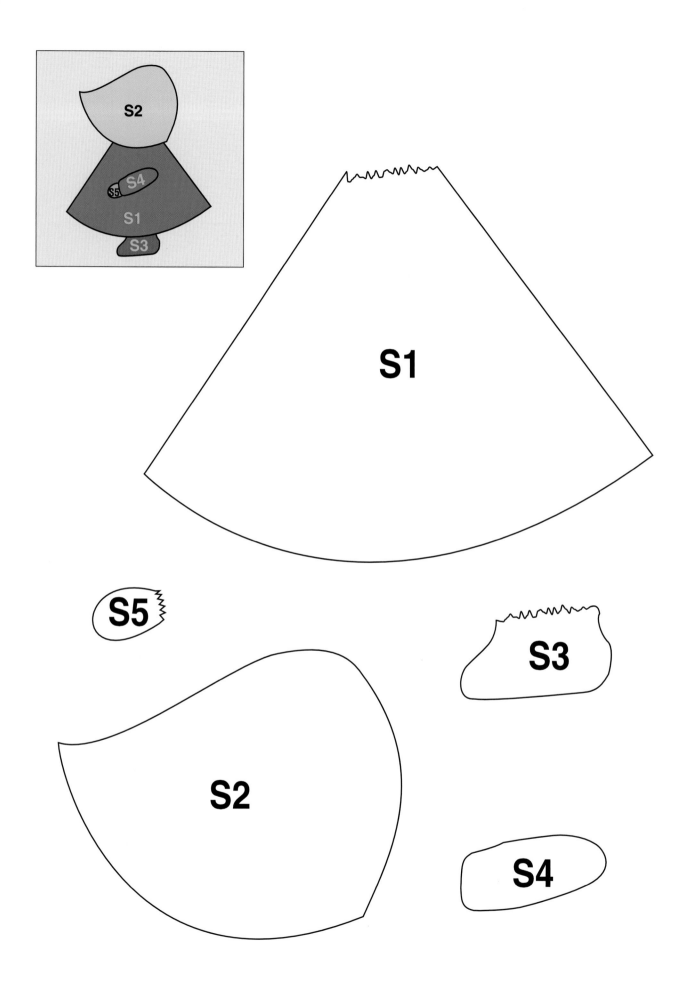

S2

S4
S5
S1
S3

S1

S5

S3

S2

S4

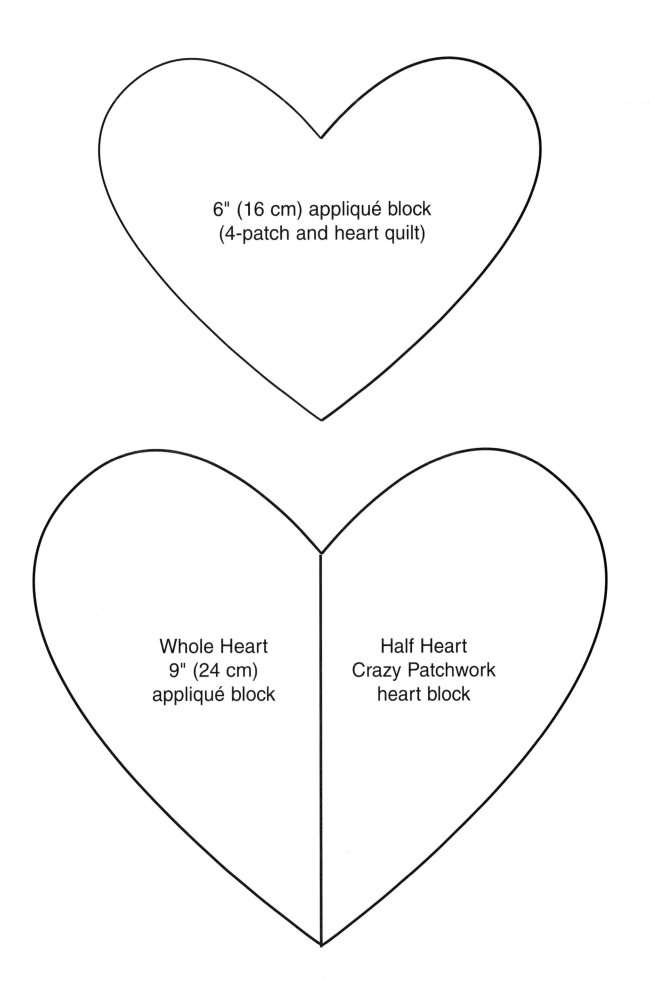

6" (16 cm) appliqué block
(4-patch and heart quilt)

Whole Heart
9" (24 cm)
appliqué block

Half Heart
Crazy Patchwork
heart block

Supply Sources

Fabric
David Textiles
5959 Telegraph Rd.
City of Commerce, CA 90040
(213) 728-8231
(800) 548-1818

P & B Textiles
1580 Gilbreth Rd.
Burlingame, CA 94010
(415) 692-0422
(800) 227-6338

NW Textiles (Kona Cottons)
2509 W. Dravus
Seattle, WA 98199

Batting, Steam-a-Seam 2
The Warm Co.
954 East Union St.
Seattle, WA 98122
(206) 320-9276
(800) 234-WARM

Rotary Cutters, Mats, Scissors
Olfa Products Group
1536 Beech St.
Terre Haute, IN 47804

Rulers
Omnigrid
PO Box 663
Burlington, WA 98233
(800) 755-3530

Fabric Paint
Deka Quality Products
30 Jonathan Way
Washington Crossing, PA 18977
(213) 493-1327

Fabric Markers (Marvy)
Uchida of America
3535 Del Amo Boulevard
Torrance, CA 90503
(310) 793-2200
(800) 541-5877

Fabric Crayons (dye sticks)
Pentel of America Ltd.
2805 Columbia St.
Torrance, CA 90509
(310) 320-3831

Embroidery Floss, Needles
DMC Corp.
10 Port Kearny
South Kearny, NJ 07032
(201) 589-0606

Thread
Coats & Clark
30 Patewood Drive, Suite 351
Greenville, SC 29615
(864) 234-0331

Decorative Charms
Creative Beginnings
475 Morro Bay Blvd.
Morro Bay, CA 93442

Safety-Kut
Daniel Smith
4150 1st Avenue South
PO Box 84268
Seattle, WA 98124
(800) 426 7923

Bibliography

Useful Quilting Books and Historical References

Duke, Dennis, and Deborah Harding (Eds.). *America's Glorious Quilts*. New York: Park Lane, 1987.

Fons, Marianne, and Liz Porter. *Quilter's Complete Guide*. Birmingham, AL: Oxmoor House, Inc., and Leisure Arts, Inc., 1993.

Kiracofe, Roderick with Mary Elizabeth Johnson. *The American Quilt - A History of Cloth and Comfort 1750-1950*. New York: Clarkson N. Potter, Inc., 1993.

Laury, Jean Ray. *Imagery on Fabric*. Lafayette, CA: C and T Publishing, 1992.

Leman, Bonnie, and Judy Martin. *Log Cabin Quilts*. Wheatridge, CO: Moon over the Mountain Publishing Co., 1980.

Marsha McCloskey's Guide to Rotary Cutting (Revised). Seattle, WA: Feathered Star Productions, 1993.

Martin, Nancy. *Threads of Time*. Bothell, WA: That Patchwork Place, Inc., 1990.

McClun, Diana and Laura Nownes. *Quilts, Quilts, Quilts – The Complete Guide to Quilt Making*. Gualala, CA: The Quilt Digest, 1988.

Nelson, Cyril, and Carter Houck. *Treasury of American Quilts*. New York: Greenwich House, 1982.

Noble, Maurine. *Machine Quilting Made Easy!* Bothell, WA: That Patchwork Place, Inc., 1994.

Rolfe, Margaret with Beryl Hodges and Judy Turner. *Metric Quiltmaking*. Rozelle, New South Wales: Sally Milner Publishing, 1993.

von Gwinner, Schnuppe. *The History of the Patchwork Quilt - Origins, Traditions and Symbols of Textile Art*. West Chester, PA: Schiffer Pub. Ltd., 1988.

Walter, Cindy. *Snippet Sensations*. Iola, WI: Krause Publications, 1999.

Books With Quilting Projects for Children and Related Activities

ABC Quilts. *Kids Making Quilts for Kids*. Quilt Digest, 1992.

Amor, Jennifer. *Flavor Quilts for Kids to Make*. American Quilt Society, 1991.

Benner, Cheryl. *An Amish Quilt Coloring Book*. Good Books, 1994.

Bolton, Janet. *Mrs. Noah's Patchwork Quilt*. Andrews & McMeel, 1995.

Bolton, Janet. *My Grandmother's Patchwork Quilt*. Delacorte Press, 1993.

Cherry, Winky. *My First Patchwork Book, Hand and Machine Sewing*. Parmer Pletsch, 1997.

Cherry, Winky. *My First Quilting Book, Machine Sewing*. Parmer Pletsch, 1997.

Cobb, Mary. Illus. by Ellis, Jan Davey. *The Quilt-Block History of Pioneer Days*. Millbrook, 1995.

Eikmeier, Barbara J. *Kids Can Quilt*. That Patchwork Place, 1997.

LoPinta, Celia. *Stitch me a Story, A Guide to Children's Books with a Quilting Theme*. 1999 Obtainable from Celia LoPinta, 3044 Franklin Street, San Fransisco, CA 94123.

Smith, Nancy and Milligan, Lynda. *I'll Teach Myself 3. Step Into Patchwork*. Dreamspinners, Possibilities, 1994.

Stout, LuAnn. *Rail Fence Quilt: For Kids at Heart*. Quilt in a Day, 1993.

Willing, Karen and Dock, Julie. *Fabric Fun for Kids: Step-by-Step Projects for Children*. Now and Then Publications, 1997.

About the Author

Maggie Ball is a native of Northumberland, England. After studying biology and geography at the University of Exeter, she lived in Oxford with her husband Nigel and worked as an academic administrator. In 1986, they moved to Arkansas, where Maggie discovered quilts and was thrilled to see them displayed on clotheslines outside farmhouses on the back roads in the Ozarks. She soon began quilting and joined the local quilt group.

Maggie became president of the Arkansas Quilters' Guild in 1992. This group includes several exceptionally talented quilters whose innovative approaches to both traditional and contemporary quilting were inspiring and influential. Here Maggie organized her first classroom quilt projects with second graders at her children's school.

Since 1993, Maggie and Nigel and their two children Hazel and Thomas, have lived on Bainbridge Island near Seattle in the Pacific Northwest. Maggie has quilted with over 800 Island children, helping them to create more than 50 quilts. She teaches quilting to all ages, enjoys making art quilts, and has had her quilts exhibited both locally and nationally.

From Quilting To Crafting ...
Krause Books Have Projects For Everyone

Kaye Wood's Strip-Cut Quilts
by Kaye Wood
Learn timesaving techniques for accurate cutting and quilting with renowned quilter Kaye Wood. Explore the many triangle shapes that can be cut with the Starmaker® 8 Master Template including horizontal and vertical cuts, fussy cuts, flying geese, trees and many more. Use these shapes to create 25 beautiful projects including quilts, wall hangings, and table runners. Both beginning and advanced quilters will love Kaye Wood's easy strip-cutting techniques.
Softcover • 8-1/4 x 10-7/8 • 96 pages
200 illustrations • 30 color photos
Item# KWNSQ • $19.95

Photo Art & Craft
by Carolyn Vosburg Hall
This innovative approach to creative photography and crafting is the ultimate idea book! Filled with foolproof techniques for using tools such as photocopiers and computers, this guide shows you how to turn pictures of your family, friends, pets, landscapes, and special memories into treasured keepsakes and works of art. Includes 50 one-of-a-kind projects, like coasters, blocks, note cards, jewelry, photo frames, a quilt, lampshade, clock, and table.
Softcover • 8-1/4 x 10-7/8 • 128 pages
50 illustrations • 250 color photos
Item# PHTC • $21.95

Quick Quilted Miniatures
by Darlene Zimmerman
Create miniature quilts simply and quickly using the tips and techniques provided in this book. The author leads you through more than 35 miniature quilt designs. Colors and designs mimic décor, holidays and occasions occurring throughout the year. Featuring 40 color photographs and 140 illustrations, the book offers basic cutting and assembly information, step-by-step instructions, and tips on choosing and organizing fabric, drafting your own designs and appliqué basics.
Softcover • 8-1/4 x 10-7/8
128 pages
40 color photos & 140 illustrations
Item# QQM • $21.95

More than Memories
The Complete Guide For Preserving Your Family History
edited by Julie Stephani
Leading scrapbook experts share hundreds of their favorite tips and techniques to instruct and inspire you to create beautiful family albums that will be cherished for generations to come! Clear step-by-step instructions show you how to organize, protect, and display your treasured photos.
Softcover • 8-1/2 x 11 • 128 pages
225 color photos
Item# MTM • $14.95

Essentially Soap
The Elegant Art of Handmade Soap Making, Scenting, Coloring, & Shaping
by Dr. Robert S. McDaniel
Make "custom-made" soap with just the right scent, emollients, and eye-appeal. With Dr. Robert McDaniel's simple instructions and numerous recipes, you can make soap to match your decor, soothe your jangled nerves at the end of a hectic day, or energize you in the morning. McDaniel teaches you how to work with fragrances, skin treatments, colors, and shapes and discusses the aromatherapy benefits associated with many essential oils.
Softcover • 8-1/4 x 10-7/8
128 pages
100 color photos
Item# SOAP • $19.95

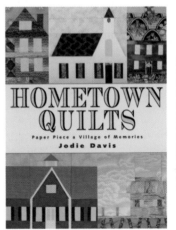

Hometown Quilts
Paper Piece a Village of Memories
by Jodie Davis
Create your own hometown quilt using paper piecing and any combination of the 27 block patterns included in this easy-to-follow book. Complete step-by-step illustrated instructions and full-size patterns are used to teach paper piece quilting, one of the hottest techniques among quilters today. Clear layout diagrams and beautiful color photographs will inspire you to create a quilt from the book, or come up with your own village of memories.
Softcover • 8-1/4 x 10-7/8 • 128 pages
50 color photos
Item# MEMQU • $21.95